IMMIGRANT SECRETS

IMMIGRANT SECRETS

The Search for My Grandparents

JOHN MANCINI

All Rights Reserved, Copyright 2022 by John F. Mancini
2nd edition

No part of this book may be reproduced or transmitted in any form or by any means, graphic, electronic, or mechanical, including photocopying, recording, taping, or by any information storage or retrieval system, without permission.

Web visitors welcomed—and encouraged!—as are reviews on Amazon.
Help me spread the word.
http://www.SearchforMyGrandparents.com

ISBN: 979-8-218-01856-6

For my parents.

We look to the stories of our origins to make sense of things, to remember who we are.
The role of origin stories...is to enlighten the present by recalling the past.
Origin stories are rarely straightforward history. Over the years, they morph into a colorful amalgam of truth and myth, nostalgia and cautionary tale, the shades of their significance brought out by the particular light of a particular moment.

—Rachel Held Evans

FAMILY TREE 1.0

MY FATHER
- Joseph John Mancini (1925–1987)

MY MOTHER
- Sallyann Theresa Manson (1931–)

MY SIBLINGS
- June (1956–), Joe (1958–), Jennifer (1959–), Jeff (1963–), Jeanne (1966–)

MY MATERNAL GRANDPARENTS
- John Oliver Manson (1880–1945)
- Sarah Anne McEvoy (1892–1967)

MY MOTHER'S SIBLINGS
- John Francis Manson, half-brother (1913–1979)
- Marcia Evangeline Manson, half-sister (1923–2000)
- Douglas John Manson (1930–1994)

MY PATERNAL GRANDPARENTS
- Frank Mancini (unknown–c. 1930)
- Elizabeth DeFabritus (unknown–c. 1930)

MY FATHER'S SIBLINGS
- Vincent George Mancini (1928–?)

PROLOGUE

JOSEPH JOHN MANCINI (1925-1987)
Joseph gazed at the lights, lights that offered promise. And peace. Lights that offered home.

As he drifted toward the lights, his speed was both inconceivably fast, and at the same time agonizingly slow. He had always known of these lights, but they were always somewhere deep within himself and beyond his grasp.

All that was changing now. He prayed that he would know and be known.

And then the lights vanished. Just vanished.

I stare at the keyboard, not quite clear where to start this strange project.

My ninth-grade English teacher, Miss Porro, used to say, "Just tell them what you're going to tell them. Tell them. Tell them what you told them."

In retrospect this was hardly unique advice in high school English classes. But it struck a chord at the time, even though

Miss Porro's long-term commitment to education might have been suspect after she reportedly ran off to join the Country Bear Jamboree at Disney World shortly after the school year ended.

So. "Tell them what you're going to tell them."

This is an "origins" story. Specifically, it's a story about the "origins" of my family.

I'm not sure where my sudden interest in my family roots came from, but it has become an obsession that won't quite go away. Perhaps it was after becoming a grandparent, when I realized there is a strange and tenuous connection between generations. The realization that there is an underlying and continuing story that is useful in understanding our own story. That there is power in being part of a bigger story, a story connected both to what was and what will be. And that there are voices that need to be heard and stories that need to be told.

It's only with the connection to our own grandchildren—a connection with none of those pesky parental expectations, just pure, unfiltered love—that I realized something was missing when we were growing up. I only had one-quarter of a full grandparent contingent of four. My grandmother, Sarah Anne McEvoy from Conaslee, Ireland, was the only grandparent I ever knew. I knew *of* my maternal grandfather, John Oliver Manson, but that was about it. He died in 1945.

Like many of their greatest generation compadres, my parents, Joseph and Sallyann, quickly headed for the suburbs shortly after they were married. They arrived in New Jersey, and began their own personal population explosion, having six kids—John, June, Joseph, Jennifer, Jeffrey, and Jeanne—within an eleven-year span. Yes, all Js. It was a typical story of life in the suburbs. Imagine the *Wonder Years* set in New Jersey, and you can get the picture. I would like to say that my role was Kevin Arnold, but truth be told, I was more of a Paul Pfeiffer.

On the *Wonder Years*, you always had a feeling there was some untold story concerning Kevin's father Jack and *his* father. Bit by bit over the years, the backstory is revealed. Kevin's father was born in 1927. He grew up during the Great Depression, served in the US Marine Corps during the Korean War, and worked as a product distribution manager at NORCOM, a somewhat mysterious large military defense company. Later, he started his own business building and selling handcrafted furniture. In the last episode, it was revealed that he died of a heart attack in 1975.

There are certain parallels. My father was born in 1925. He grew up during the Great Depression, served in the US

Navy during WWII and worked as a business analyst at Union Carbide, a somewhat mysterious large chemical company. Later, he started his own business with a friend, but I have no idea what they did. In my father's last episode, he had a heart attack in New York City in 1987 shortly after officially retiring. He survived in a coma for another week or so and lasted until the day after my wife gave birth to our son William. I guess he wanted to make sure everything turned out OK with William.

There is one significant difference between Jack Arnold in the *Wonder Years* and my father. Jack's father and Kevin's grandfather, Albert Arnold, is a recurring character in the series. He has a bit of a difficult relationship with his son. In one episode, Albert buys Kevin a dog named Buster and in another one he sells Kevin his car for a dollar. Kevin's grandfather is a widower; his grandmother appears only in flashbacks. His grandfather is a cantankerous character, but there is evidently an extended family out there; one episode features a rather grim family car trip to go to the funeral of a cousin named Rose.

There was nothing like this rich background story in our own New Jersey version of the *Wonder Years*. To put it bluntly, there was no backstory for my father.

The Chinese consider ancestors and their ghosts or spirits to be part of this world. They are neither supernatural (in the sense of being outside nature) nor transcendent in the sense of being beyond nature. Ancestors are humans who have become godly beings, who keep their individual identities and who stay alive through the stories of their descendants.

In our family, we have many fine attributes, but curiosity about this strange vacuum of Italian ancestors was not one of them. I don't really know my father's full story. Who was he, really? Why the silence about his family?

My father, Joseph Mancini, was a man who loved a joke and who didn't mind being the butt of a joke. We once convinced him to wear my Ramapo High School band uniform and put on an Oscar worthy performance of a street sweeper (a "Strassenputzer"—likely the sum total of three years of high school German) with many mouths to feed. He even allowed my buddy Ron and me to gather all the kids in the neighborhood for the photo shoot. It was for a German class video and shot on 8 mm film. I can tell endless stories about my father and the crazy things he did.

My father used to joke that during the years he commuted into New York City from New Jersey he would "leave his brain at the office" and not notice *anything* that occurred between home and the Union Carbide Building on Park Avenue in New York. He said he kept work in one box and home in another, and anything that occurred in between was just a mystery to him.

I got to experience this one summer when we both worked at Union Carbide. We would take the train into Hoboken, then the Path tubes to 33rd Street, and then walk—Lord, he could walk fast—the twelve north-south blocks and five, long east-west blocks, and usually arrive like clockwork at around 8:30. I would like to say that we used this time to bond deeply and discuss important issues, but truth be told, I was mostly half asleep and/or looking at girls, and he was, well, in his own self-confessed interim space in which *nothing* registered between home and Park and 47th.

His incredible skills of both avoidance and focus were demonstrated to me one morning as we walked up 6th Avenue. Looking ahead, I noticed a six-foot, six-inch man coming toward us, wearing purple high-top sneakers and nothing else. He seemed to accelerate as he approached, ultimately walking directly in between the two of us.

As we continued past our chance encounter with the purple high-top man, everyone he had left in his wake was, of course, pointing and laughing. It was a strange sight even in 1970s New York. My father stirred a bit from whatever internal conversation he was having.

"What is everyone looking at?" he asked.

He hadn't seen it. Nothing. Nada. The at-home world and the at-work world were in their boxes, with the daily trip to and from New York somewhat of a no-man's land between the two worlds.

My father would go to any lengths to avoid conflict. The phrase, "We just won't go there anymore" was used so often and in so many contexts in our family that it became something of a legend. If we had been older, it would have been good fodder for a drinking game, a game that he would have refused to play.

It may sound like we all collectively suffered from the most pathetic lack of curiosity about my father's family, but every family has its blank spots. And my father's family was ours.

Without any memory of my father's parents, I sometimes wonder if they even existed. If their lives went unrecorded and forgotten, what then? What did it mean to my father to have this void in his life? What did it mean to us to be missing half our family? We didn't know *anything* about them other than their names and a few very sketchy details. What does it mean to have no ancestors to honor or remember? I don't know if it matters to the rest of the family, but it matters to me.

Truth be told, I think we were oblivious to this void growing up. After all, there were a lot of us to keep each other occupied; we were only one player short of a baseball team. There are many families that have gaps in what they know about their origins. But perhaps we were a bit over the top in this regard.

I wonder why we never knew more.

I realize now that I was dodging the core issue when I started this project. So, let me formally restate the "tell them what you are going to tell them" challenge from Miss Porro with regards to this story:

> This is the story of the search for my father's mystery parents. And in telling their story, I hope to better understand my father's story.

The story in this book of the search itself is a rather typical family history journey, albeit one that revealed things I never could have imagined about our family. One thing I found along this journey is that genealogy people are incredibly helpful. I spent a good portion of the last twenty-plus years of my career hanging about with records managers and archivists. I will admit that in the rush to embrace the latest and greatest technology, I didn't always understand or appreciate them. But I do now. Any errors in genealogy are not intentional. But they are my fault.

The story in this book of my Italian grandparents is in fact a *story*. But it is, as they say in the movie industry, "based on a true story." The facts that surround the story of Elizabeth and Frank are true, but the color and texture that surround those facts are my own creations to give them life. As Christian columnist and *New York Times* bestselling author Rachel Held Evans said in her 2018 book *Inspired: Slaying Giants, Walking on Water, and Loving the Bible Again*, "Origin stories are rarely straightforward history. Over the years, they morph into a colorful amalgam of truth and myth, nostalgia and cautionary tale."

As to what this all means about my father's story—Dad you'll need to trust me for a bit; I did my best. We see each other dimly now through a lot of years and a lot of unknowns, but someday we'll sit down together, and all will be known.

ONE

It was late at night in 1987 when the phone rang. I was not expecting a call and had a bad feeling when I answered it. "I'm afraid I have bad news," my mother said when I picked up the receiver. "Your father went into the city as usual this morning, and then just didn't come home. It took a while to track him down. I called some of his coworkers and then the state police, but they knew nothing. You know how he's usually reliable as clockwork. I finally called the local police, and they eventually tracked him down."

My head nodded methodically as a sense of dread rose by the second.

"He apparently had a heart attack on the way to his first appointment, and he got separated from his wallet, which is why it took so long to track him down. He's alive, but in a coma at Bellevue Hospital in Manhattan."

"OK. I'll be there tomorrow." That's how I found myself on the Amtrak, headed up to New York a week *after* the due date for our second child, but *before* child number two decided to make his formal appearance. I planned to go up and back on the same day, one foot headed to New York to be with my father in a coma, and the other foot still firmly rooted in Herndon and waiting for labor to begin.

Bellevue was . . . well it was chaotic for a suburban kid. In a bit of fog, I stared at the mission statement on the message board at the main entrance: "Bellevue is America's oldest operating hospital, established in 1736 . . . Our mission is to provide the highest quality of care to New York's population and to deliver health care to every patient with dignity, cultural sensitivity and compassion, regardless of ability to pay."

All the way up on the train, the name Bellevue kept picking at my consciousness. Why was this name so familiar? I had never been there, and yet some sort of familiarity kept pushing through. As I stared at the inspiring mission statement—and thought about the fact that this place had been there for 250 years—it came to me. Bellevue. Growing up in the shadow of New York I couldn't believe it had taken me the entire train ride—plus the chaos in the lobby—to remember: Bellevue was where the crazy people were.

Though Bellevue is now a full-service hospital, it was once popularly associated with the treatment of mentally ill patients who required psychiatric commitment. The name "Bellevue" was shorthand in the New York area—even across the country—for lunatic asylum. As David Oshinsky wrote in *Bellevue: Three Centuries of Medicine and Mayhem at America's Most Storied Hospital*,

> You can't factor out Bellevue as a psychiatric hospital. When I was growing up as a kid in New York City, when I was acting weird my mother would say, "Keep it up and you're going to Bellevue." It was like a national punch line.

This was the place where author Norman Mailer was taken after he stabbed his wife. This was the place where Mark David Chapman was brought after he shot John Lennon. This was the place mentioned by name by Allen Ginsberg in his poem "Howl," and where he was a patient. High school English came in handy for something after all.

Of course, this is not the way we talk about mental illness today, and I am not making light of mental illness. But I can hear my parents now, "Keep it up kids, and we'll all wind up in Bellevue."

Be careful what you wish for.

By the time I arrived from DC, things had gone downhill with my father. He was still in a coma. The doctors told my mother, "Things don't look good; there doesn't seem to be evidence of brain activity." My father would have had a field day with that after all the jokes he made over the years about leaving his brain at the office.

He looked peaceful. Frankly, he looked good. He looked like he was planning the most incredible practical joke ever. "I *told* you we would all wind up in Bellevue!"

My sister Jeanne had taken a flight back from college. "The man sitting next to me on the plane was a businessman," she told me. "He had a suit and tie on. And he asked me why I was going to New Jersey, and I told him and then I started sobbing and sobbing. And he was the nicest man and he kept saying that things would be alright and hugged me when I got off the plane."

But I knew just looking at my dad that this was not going to end well. I don't remember this, but my sister Jennifer says that someone was handcuffed in the bed next to my father in the ICU, and there was a guard. My brother Joseph remembers that a patient periodically wandered into the waiting room looking in the ashtrays (yes, you could smoke in a hospital waiting room at the time) for unfinished cigarette butts. To add to the charm, the pants on the cigarette seeker were only loosely gathered around his waist and kept falling down. Not good signs.

So many things ran through my head. Just two months earlier—our last out-of-town trip before the "no more trips" part of pregnancy—we had been home to New Jersey. We had all been standing on the back deck, and my father was bouncing up and down, up and down, on a portable trampoline. My mother's words echoed in my mind, "Joe, be careful. You'll have a heart attack." Sigh.

While I went through the motions of pleading with God for a miracle, to grant this funny and quirky man a sudden, last-minute reprieve from the Grim Reaper, in my heart of hearts I knew it was not to be. I thanked him for being a great father. I uttered a few curses that it had to come to this, at age 62. I hoped he heard me. I kept waiting for some unexpected twitch or eyeblink to signify that he knew I was there, but it was not to be.

As I left the room, and looked back at him just lying there under a sheet, I knew I would not see him again. That he would never meet his new grandchild. That I would never get to ask him all the things I should have asked him, but never did, assuming time would extend out forever. Or at least for a while longer. Except that it didn't.

After a few hours, I left Bellevue, hoping to never hear of this place again, and went back to DC.

A few days later, our son William was born. The day after that, my father died. Even though all the machines were showing flat-lined brain activity, my sister Jennifer says that after my mom told him about William, a tear rolled down his face.

On the death certificate, under parents, it lists Frank and Elizabeth Mancini.

So many questions.

Normally, my business trips are functional. Fly in somewhere. Go to a hotel. Give a speech. Fly home. But for my trip to Iowa in 2000, once I found out that the Field of Dreams was only sixty-one miles away—the iconic baseball field built next to an Iowa corn field in the movie by the same name, in which Ray Kinsella is urged by a mysterious voice to build a baseball field in part of his cornfield in the hopes of fulfilling a dream—I knew I must go. Even if it meant an extra overnight stop.

All the way up, driving through endless fields of corn, I marveled at how amazingly dark it is out in the middle of the country. It was "inside your pocket" dark. I started to worry a bit about the stories that might arise if I should slam into some cow suddenly crossing in front of me in the middle of all this darkness at sixty miles per hour. I couldn't remember if I told anyone I was indulging in this diversion, and now I found myself on this lonely stretch of highway, driving *away* from the place where I was scheduled to give my speech.

Fortunately, I encountered no cows and pulled into the parking lot at the Colonial Inn. Probably unnecessarily, I had made a reservation, and someone was waiting up for me to give me the key. The room was only $29 per night, with wire hangers in the "closet" area included at no extra charge.

I woke up the next morning still a bit surprised that I had made this trip. It was quite foggy, and I decided to wait out the fog. Truth be told, I was not quite sure what I would find when I got to my destination, which is why I was dragging my feet. A core Mancini family value is a fear of looking foolish, and it dawned on me that when I tell people where I have gone, they will think I am nuts.

After I stopped at a diner and consumed at least 1000 calories, I decided that I could not procrastinate any longer. According to my printed directions—this was a pre-MapQuest, pre-GPS era—my quest was just four miles away. In the movie, the character Terrence Mann (played by James Earl Jones) is a frustrated and alienated writer looking to find the idealism that vanished in the wave of success that followed his early books. His voice came to me during my hesitation:

> People will come, Ray. They'll come to Iowa for reasons they can't even fathom. They'll turn up your driveway not knowing for sure why they're doing it. They'll arrive at your door as innocent as children, longing for the past (Robinson, Phil, dir. 1989. *Field of Dreams*. Los Angeles: Universal Pictures).

And suddenly I arrived at the Field of Dreams. For reasons I could not even fathom.

I was the only one there. There was no admission fee, no gate. Just a curious trailer-esque souvenir stand that was not quite open yet. Other than that, it was just like walking directly into the movie. I was surprised at how faithful this place was to the peacefulness of the movie, that it had not been turned into some marketing machine. At least not yet. I guessed it would not survive in this condition forever.

It was, well, just a baseball field. A small backstop, a field, and lights. The outfield was bordered by corn, a living home run barrier around the perimeter of the outfield. Aside the field between home plate and first base were the small bleachers that are the setting for much of the action in the movie. A couple of hundred yards behind the bleachers sat the beautiful white country house with its wraparound porch and the famous porch swing where you could sit in the twilight hours when the fireflies came out, for those moments when it seemed that all was well with the world. I stared out at the edge of the cornfield, a place where the lines seemed to blur between what was real and what could be.

Moonlight Graham was a minor league ball player who got the opportunity to play one game in the major leagues. He was played by Burt Lancaster in the movie. I recalled Lancaster's most famous line in the movie:

> We just don't recognize life's most significant moments while they're happening. Back then I thought, "Well, there'll be other days." I didn't realize that that was the only day (Robinson 1989).

After coming on this strange side trip, I realized I was hoping that this might not be just one of those "other" days. Not just another of those mindless fly-sleep-eat-speak-fly business trips. Perhaps it could be one of *those* days. As the James Earl Jones character (Terrance Mann) wrote, "There comes a time when all the cosmic tumblers have clicked into place and the universe opens itself up for a few seconds to show you what is possible."

Yeah, perhaps I was expecting a bit much from a visit to a small town in eastern Iowa.

Just as my latent cynicism was about to rear its head, I noticed a guest book, and started to leaf through the pages.

> My father and I are meeting here today after not speaking to each other for 15 years. Wish me luck.
> I hadn't even seen the movie when my kids arranged this trip and told me to bring a baseball glove. I thought they were nuts. They were not.

> I hope that something magical will happen when I go out into the corn. I could really use it right now.

> We brought our gloves and just stood in the infield throwing the ball around. I had seen the movie, the kids had not. They couldn't understand why I was crying.

> I'm starting chemo tomorrow. I just sat on those little bleachers for an hour. It felt like I was glued to the spot. I just stared at the field, and the bus load of tourists from Minneapolis just faded into the background. For a few moments, I was 12 years old and back at the Polo Grounds.

Page after page after page of people pouring out their hearts. What a strange place.

During the movie, the mysterious players who come every day to play on Ray Kinsella's field miraculously appear and disappear from the corn that borders right field. The players just slowly emerge from the corn when it's time to play, and slowly disappear when the day is done. The edge of the corn field is the tipping point at which the cosmic tumblers click into place.

Terrance Mann is determined to find out what happens in that cornfield.

> Ray. Ray. Listen to me, Ray. Listen to me. There is something out there, Ray, and if I have the courage to go through with this, what a story it'll make (Robinson 1989).

In a moment of pure irrationality, I decided what the hell; I was going to walk out to the cornfield and see if anything happened. Like the characters in the movie, I slowly eased up to the right field corn wall and poked my head in tentatively. I looked back to see if anyone else had arrived and was witness to my foolishness. No one was here. OK.

I stepped into the corn. Nothing. I stepped in a few steps more. I came back out of the corn into right field and tried again. In. Out. In. Out. Maybe there was a trick to this. Nothing.

Truth be told, I never fully expected that I could enter the movie and that my father would actually appear and offer to have a catch with me, although I think I had hoped for at least a glimpse into what lay beyond the corn. A glimpse of what his life had meant, of what he had hoped his life would be, and whether he was at peace.

But alas, while I still retained some of the warm fuzzies from the guest book, this was not to be a day for cosmic tumblers. I headed back to the parking lot, and stopped for a souvenir mug at the trailer, a mug featuring the characters from the movie standing amidst the corn. The package said that when you added hot liquid to the cup, the characters disappeared into the corn. That's at least something, I guess.

I hopped into the rental car and headed back the sixty miles to Cedar Rapids for my speech. Thoughts of my father surrounded me in a cloud. Perhaps the field had worked some sort of magic after all, just not exactly what I expected.

"Ease his pain."

TWO

Every year at Cape Hatteras, I go on a bike ride along a somewhat fixed path, one that goes first to the Cape Hatteras lighthouse, then past a tiny World War II British cemetery, and from there to a National Park Service campground immediately prior to Beach Access Ramp 43. There is a mile-and-a-quarter road that rings the campground, and at the end of my ten-mile campground velodrome, I head back north toward Route 12. But I first ride out an abandoned road that goes about a third of a mile, almost to the dunes.

On this day, at the end of the abandoned road, I arrive at what I somewhat jokingly refer to as my own meditation point, mainly to hide my routine from those who might think me nuts or overly religious (even though, truth be told, I tend to be both). I pause and look around at the gray bones of trees long dead from ocean over wash and gather my thoughts.

I reflect a bit on the fact that I have now officially lived one day longer than the 22,834 days accorded to my father. I realize that I am now officially in uncharted territory. The statute of limitations on being your father's son never quite runs out, but it certainly takes on a different feel once you live longer than he did. It is in that moment that I decide to see what I can find out about my father's parents.

Before I dive into the task of finding my mysterious paternal grandparents, I decide it might be best to sharpen my skills by researching and writing down what I know about my mother's parents. My maternal grandmother, Sarah McEvoy, was the only grandparent I ever knew personally, and she was quite a piece of work.

I activate my Ancestry.com account and plunge in to see what I can add to what I already know about her story.

My grandmother was born on 4 February 1892 in a townland called Graigueafulla, in Clonaslee district in Queens County, which was rechristened Laois County after British-themed place-naming became somewhat unfashionable in Ireland.

I find Sarah in the 1901 census in Ireland. It is good here to have some sort of verification of her age, because my great aunts and grandmother had a notorious habit of lying about their ages. This tended to have a somewhat cascading effect on everyone else's ages since they were all bunched so closely together. And Sarah's name is not the only one to show up. There are a baker's dozen plus one of McEvoys that make their presence known in the 1901 census: father, Martin; mother, Kate; Martin's sister Sarah; and kids: Patrick, Martin, Joseph, Edward, Mary, Margaret, Sarah, Michael, Kate, Elizabeth, and George. One sibling, John, died at age five from "paralysis" on 2 May 1889 before Sarah was born.

NAME and SURNAME		RELATION to Head of Family	RELIGIOUS PROFESSION	EDUCATION	AGE		SEX
Christian Name	Surname				Years on last Birthday	Months for Infants under one Year	
Martin	McEvoy	Head of Family	Catholic	Read and Write	58		M
Kate	McEvoy	Wife	Catholic	Read and Write	43		F
Sarah	McEvoy	Sister	Catholic	Read	56		F
Patrick	McEvoy	Son	Catholic	Read and Write	20		M
Martin	McEvoy	Son	Catholic	Read and Write	18		M
Joseph	McEvoy	Son	Catholic	Read and Write	15		M
Edward	McEvoy	Son	Catholic	Read and Write	14		M
Mary	McEvoy	daughter	Catholic	Read and Write	12		F
Margret	McEvoy	daughter	Catholic	Read and Write	11		F
Sarah	McEvoy	daughter	Catholic	Read and Write	9		F
Michael	McEvoy	Son	Catholic	cannot Read	8		M
Kate	McEvoy	daughter	Catholic	cannot Read	7		F
Elizabeth	McEvoy	daughter	Catholic	cannot Read	4		F
George	McEvoy	Son	Catholic	cannot Read	1		M

I wonder how all these kids were conceived when I look at the secondary census form. According to that form, their house had three rooms and three windows in the front of the house, so privacy for these fourteen people must have been a somewhat comical concern. But I guess where there's a will, there's a way. They also had a stable, a cow house, a piggery (cool name), and a chicken coop.

By the time of the 1911 Irish census, things had changed a bit. In terms of the animals, things were looking up. There was a stable, but now there were two cow houses, one for cows and one for calves, and three piggeries. I'm not sure how that breaks down into actual pigs. Plus, they had two chicken coops, a shed, and a barn. The animals were living high.

Not so good on the human side. The number of people in the house in 1911 was down from fourteen to eight: father, Martin; mother, Kate; Edward; Mary; Sarah; Michael; Kate; and Elizabeth.

NAME AND SURNAME.		RELATION to Head of Family.	RELIGIOUS PROFESSION.	EDUCATION.	AGE (last Birthday) and SEX.	
Christian Name.	Surname.				Ages of Males.	Ages of Females.
1.	2.	3.	4.	5.	6.	7.
Martin	McEvoy	Head of family	Roman Catholic	Read and write	46 yrs	
Catherine	McEvoy	Wife	,,	Read and write		53 yrs
Edward	McEvoy	Son	,,	Read and write	24 yrs	
Mary	McEvoy	Daughter	,,	Read & write		21 yrs
Sarah	McEvoy	Daughter	,,	Read & write		19 yrs
Michael	McEvoy	Son	,,	Read & write	17 yrs	
Katie	McEvoy	Daughter	,,	Read & write		15 yrs
Lizzie	McEvoy	Daughter	,,	Read & write		13 yrs

What happened to the rest of them?

- Sarah's aunt, for whom she must have been named, died sometime between the 1901 census and 1911 census.
- Sarah's little brother George (one year old at the time of the previous census) died on 6 August 1902 at three years old, probably from spinal disease and secondary paralysis.
- Patrick, the oldest in the family, died on 13 November 1905 at twenty-four from asthma complications.
- Sarah's older sister Margaret left for America on 4 June 1908 from Queenstown aboard the SS *Umbria*).
- Her brother Joseph left a year later, 26 August 1909, aboard the SS *Teutonic*.
- Still to come, her brother Martin would die in 1913 at age thirty.

Fast-forward a bit, and I find Sarah on the deck of the SS *Adriatic* in 1924 headed for America. Sarah, traveling with her sister, Elizabeth, arrived in the US on 17 November 1924.

At some point in the next few years, Sarah wandered to Florida. I'm amazed at this degree of mobility for a newly arrived immigrant in 1920s America. Sarah and John Oliver Manson were married at St. Anthony's Church in Ft. Lauderdale on 13 November 1929. Astute examiners of the marriage license application will note three things: 1) My grandmother's occupation is listed as nurse, something I had never heard before; 2) They claimed that neither of them had ever been married before. This was perhaps to expedite the marriage by a Catholic priest, since divorce was still forbidden at that point; and 3) The spelling of both her first name (listed as Sara) and last name (listed as McAvoy) was apparently a variable thing.

My mother grew up in what would today be called a single-parent household, but back then they probably had some sort of other label that was not terribly attractive. I am not sure where everyone thought her father—my grandfather John—actually *was*, but he sure wasn't with the rest of the family.

My grandfather John was born in Sweden and evidently lived there through his early teenage years. Inexplicably, he seems to have always claimed Melbourne, Australia, as his birthplace on official documents once he got to the United States. I have no idea why. Family lore has it that he sailed around the world seven times. His mother died when he was two. He seems to have had three sisters, all of whom died before him. He somehow wound up in Rio at the age of seventeen, where he contracted yellow fever. He was accidentally shot in the left side in South Africa in 1898, perhaps in the Boer War (the Australians fought on the side of the English).

At one point my grandfather was well known in Florida as a sea captain. He was the winner of a famous Miami to Key West boat race, a race that his own son (my Uncle Jack) would also win years later. He was the captain of the Presidential Yacht of Warren G. Harding. To put Warren G. Harding into context for those without a background in history, Donald Trump was the modern version of Warren G. Harding, except not as smart, nor as ethical. My grandfather was married to someone other than my grandmother during this period.

My grandfather also ran booze from the Bahamas to Miami during Prohibition with seven-year-old Jack in tow. My uncle would sit on the bow of the ship as a decoy and pretend to fish. They made about twenty-five runs and deliveries until one night during a delivery he sensed a setup, threw a suitcase of booze out the window, and abruptly ended his career as a rumrunner.

My grandfather separated from his first wife in 1925, and there was apparently more than the usual amount of tension involved in the separation. In late June, he posted a notice in the *Miami Daily News* proclaiming that "he was not responsible for any debts incurred by his wife." A few weeks later, there was another series of stories reporting that my Uncle Jack had been kidnapped. The story must have made the wire services because versions of it appeared in most of the major newspapers in the Southeast over a period of two or three days and ran like this:

> Police Ask Help in Finding Youth
> Miami, July 10. Miami police today issued a country-wide appeal for Jack Manson, son of Mr. and Mrs. John O. Manson, missing since Wednesday morning. Jack is believed to have been kidnapped. A woman's voice over the telephone invited Jack to attend a party to be given by one of his school chums. Later that night Mrs. Manson learned that the telephone call had been faked (*Miami Daily News*, 10 July 1925).

A few days later, there was another round of headlines, thereby establishing a hint of some of the custody chaos that must have been in play:

> Missing Boy Safe with Dad—Mrs. Manson believes lost lad "Jack" is with Parent "Somewhere in Florida" (*Miami Daily News*)

Prior to the Great Depression, my grandfather did well for himself, so perhaps a sea captain represented something of a catch for my immigrant Irish grandmother. Unfortunately for my grandmother, their wedding date corresponded almost to the day with Black Tuesday (the day the stock market crashed). My grandfather lost everything during the crash, except his wandering spirit. My mom told stories of her father selling pencils door to door.

There was a gold stake in Nevada in the 1930s. I have an old picture of my mother, her brother, and my grandmother Sarah panning for gold. It was like something out of the *Grapes of Wrath*, shifting the scene from agriculture to the mining of precious metals.

My grandfather died in 1945 in Reno, Nevada (a good place for a risk taker) and was living at the time with a non-existent "sister." My grandmother Sarah only found out about his death through a response from the Veterans Administration after she inquired as to his whereabouts. Years later, my mother discovered he died from a self-inflicted gunshot wound when, during her own genealogy quest, she requested his military records.

My grandmother never went back to Ireland, although she did regularly buy a ticket to the Irish Sweepstakes. I grew up hearing about the Irish Sweepstakes and sometimes saw tickets for it. I often wondered exactly how you would collect on a winning ticket and when exactly the drawings were. I read later that a network of old IRA men sold the tickets and collected the proceeds.

I remember going to my grandmother's apartment in the Bronx where she lived until she died. She worked as a maid at the Barbizon Plaza Hotel in New York City for years and years. The Barbizon Plaza Hotel was located south of Columbus Circle. The property was purchased in 1981 by Donald Trump.

My grandmother was not a wealthy person, but she bought the clarinet that would set me on the path of a lifetime of loving music. She took my brother and me to Florida when I was twelve, knowing deep down that she was already suffering from the brain cancer that would kill her.

After she died, I found a copy of the *New York Daily News* from 17 August 1948, in her apartment. She kept it because it was the day that Babe Ruth died. I wonder what that was about. We had her dresser in our basement for a long time after she died. Every time you opened a drawer in that old dresser for years afterwards, you would get a vague scent of her perfume.

Armed with this information and newly confident in my Ancestry.com and Newspapers.com search skills, I decide that perhaps it is time to get serious about my father's family origins story. Where did his family go? Why didn't he ever talk about them? What happened to him after they died? How could I breathe life into the dry Ezekiel bones of my father's vanished family? Or was this a story best left untouched?

Genesis says that the earth was without form and darkness was upon the face of the deep and God simply commanded light into existence. In Hinduism, Diwali is the festival of light, a celebration of the victory of light over darkness. One of the oldest Hindu scriptures urges god to lead us into light from darkness. The Buddhists have numerous buddhas of light, including a Buddha of Boundless Light, a Buddha of Unimpeded Light, and Buddhas of Unopposed Light, of Pure Light, of Incomparable Light, and of Unceasing Light. That's a lot of Buddhas.

There was not a lot of light in my father's story.

The English word *genesis* is Greek in origin, and depending on its context, can mean "birth," "genealogy," or "history of origin." I start my Ancestry.com origins quest armed with these skeletal Mancini family facts to illuminate the void:

1. My father's parents were named Frank and Elizabeth. Her maiden name was DeFabritus.
2. They were from Italy.
3. They came to the United States in the 1920s and settled in New York City.
4. My father had a brother named Vincent.
5. My father worked in a fruit stand.

6. He served in World War II in the US Navy on the USS *Simpson*.

And one more speculative point: I always believed that my father's parents died in a fire in the 1930s. Although I was hesitant to ask my mom any questions about my search, not quite sure what she knew and what she kept hidden, I asked her straight out about the fire in the 1930s that killed my grandparents. The only thing she said was, "Where did you get this whole 'died in a fire' thing?" So, I checked with my sister June and asked if she knew how Frank and Elizabeth had died. She said, "In a fire in the 1930s." OK, check.

None of the rest of my siblings had any idea what I was talking about. We certainly don't seem to have our act together on this whole "origins story" thing.

Perhaps because I knew my maternal grandmother, I find myself drawn to focus my initial search on my father's mother, Elizabeth, and plan to use that as leverage to find out about Frank, my father's father. My first step in the quest is to find out how and *when* she got here. *Why* would be nice as well but given that we never even really knew she existed, that seems a far stretch for the Ancestry.com search engine.

I begin my Ancestry search looking for the ship that brought her to the United States. And the information pops up remarkably easily. There in front of me is the ship's manifest from the RMS *Olympic*, showing my grandmother arriving in New York at Ellis Island on 28 July 1920.

I discover that Elisabeth's hometown was Itri, a small city on the western coast of Italy about 100 kilometers north of Naples. The earliest records of Itri date to AD 914. The city was built on an ancient Roman road called the Appian Way. There was a massacre of Sardinian immigrants in Itri in 1911, provoked by fear of outsiders and job loss. Some things never change.

As I look closely at the manifest, I realize something I had overlooked. My grandmother's name was not actually Elizabeth. It was Elisabetta. I imagine she got anglicized somewhere along the way or anglicized herself in the quest to fit in.

This makes me pause. Elizabeth was always just an abstract concept to me given that the name had no context. "Elizabeth" was not quite even a name, more a word than a person. Elisabetta sounds like a real person, someone who might have actually existed.

As I think about this, it occurs to me that the naming of things carries curious weight. To name something is to give it power and identity and separateness. When we first interact with the world, we hear sounds, our parents begin to give names to the things in the world around us, including themselves. Ultimately, we become aware that there is a separateness between who we are and everything else. Our name becomes a bridge to the world around us.

Elisabetta means "pledged to God." Hello, Elisabetta.

According to the ship's manifest, Elisabetta arrived via Cherbourg, France, rather than directly from Naples. That the ship originally set out from Southampton in the United Kingdom before making a stop in Cherbourg—and that Elisabetta left to immigrate to the United States from France rather than Naples—sounds somewhat exotic.

Elisabetta was five foot six with dark hair and dark eyes. According to the manifest, she was in good health, neither "deformed" nor "crippled," and she had no "identifying marks." She was neither a polygamist nor an anarchist. And she did not advocate the overthrow of the government of the United States, which is always a good thing. Her occupation was listed as domestic, and she could read and write Italian.

Her father—Voila! A great grandfather enters our story! — was Gioacchino. Even an amateur genealogist can recognize a great-grandfather when one appears.

Elisabetta's US contact was a brother named Michele who lived at 105 East Third Street.

She was planning to stay in the US.

As I delve a bit further, I discover that she was traveling with a brother—Dominick—and his new wife, also named Elisabetta. He was a US citizen. I wonder when *he* came over.

Curiously enough, the RMS *Olympic* turns out to be a famous ship. She was part of the White Star Line and was a sister ship and virtual double to the *Titanic*. Not a good omen.

On the plus side, though, I discover that Douglas Fairbanks, Jr., and his new wife, Mary Pickford, were on the same ship, along with a teenage performer from England named Archibald Leach—who would ultimately morph into Cary Grant. I imagine, though, that all their travel accommodations were a bit different from Elisabetta's.

Meanwhile, on another ship, I find Frank, or rather Francesco. He came to the United States via Naples on 24 May 1921 aboard the SS *Pannonia*, which was built in 1904 and eventually scuttled in Hamburg in 1922.

His father's name is listed as Giuseppe; his point of contact in the US was his brother, also named Michele, eventually anglicized to Michael. Another great-grandfather revealed!

He also shared his future wife's predilections against anarchism and polygamy.

A good start for life in the United States.

I decide to get a bit adventurous and begin searching for how to find Italian military records—I had wondered whether Francesco fought in World War I. This was not nearly as easy as pushing a bunch of Ancestry.com buttons. After a lot of lot of back-forth back-forth Google Translate adventures on email, I find my grandfather's military record. In addition to discovering his military record, I learn two facts that I had not known before: 1) Francesco's middle name was *Paolo*; and 2) He won two medals—Medaglia Commemorativa Della Guerra and the Medaglia Interalleata Della Vittoria.

FAMILY TREE 2.0

MY PATERNAL GRANDPARENTS
- Francesco "Frank" Mancini (c. 1900–?)
- Elisabetta "Elizabeth" DeFabritus (c. 1900–?)

THEIR CHILDREN
- Joseph John Mancini (1925–1987)
- Vincent George Mancini (1928–2017)

FRANCESCO'S PARENTS
- Guiseppe Mancini (1865-?)
- Maria Guiseppa Saccoccio (?–?)

FRANCESCO'S SIBLINGS
- Michael Mancini (1884–1934)

ELISABETTA'S PARENTS
- Gioacchino DeFabritus (1843–1923)
- Maria Francesca Agresti (1861–1935)

ELISABETTA'S SIBLINGS
- Michael DeFabritus, half-brother (1875–1964)
- Theresa DeFabritus (1887–1975)
- Dominick DeFabritus (1891–1984)
- Maria Civita DeFabritus (1892–1960)
- Adrianna DeFabritus (1894–1957)

THREE

Dio volendo lo faro.
If God wills, I shall do this.

FRANCESCO AND ELISABETTA, 1904

The entire family—all except Michele, who had gone to America the previous year—went to the Piazza. Everyone was so excited, and Elisabetta tried so hard to stay awake for whatever was to come. But to no avail.

Elisabetta fell asleep in Teresa's arms. She loved Teresa so much, Teresa who was almost a second mother to her. Teresa, who would comfort her when all others failed. Teresa, who would slowly rock her to sleep most nights.

Just as she had fallen off to sleep, there were voices. Loud and insistent screams and yells woke her from her deep sleep. And all around her, fires. Everywhere. All over town. She began to cry.

Teresa brought Elisabetta's face close to hers to calm her and so Elisabetta could hear her above the shouting. "Tiny one, no need to be afraid," Teresa said. "It is just the bonfires of the Festa di San Giuseppe, lit to celebrate Saint Joseph." As Elisabetta watched, hundreds of tiny embers rose into the sky, creating beautiful—but temporary—constellations of light. "Look closely into the stars created by the sparks. It is said you can see the future."

She put Elisabetta down next to her and held her hand tightly. "And now, everyone will dance and sing to celebrate all fathers, starting with Giuseppe, the father of our Lord." Teresa crossed herself. "All day, my tiny one, we have been preparing the zeppole di San Giuseppe. I can taste them now. Just wait a few minutes more."

Teresa turned Elisabetta to face her and shifted Elisabetta's feet so they rested upon her own. They twirled and danced around the fire. Elisabetta watched the lights dancing off Teresa's face, round and round as if it would never stop.

Then Elisabetta saw it. Hardly discernible to anyone but her, a shadow passed over Teresa's face, and for the first time a fear of loss swept over Elisabetta, although at two and half, she had no name for this. She shivered.

Teresa sensed the change immediately and swept Elisabetta into her arms and held her close. She rocked her back and forth, slowly singing her the lullaby that Mama had sung to her many years ago.

Ninna nanna, ninna oh
Questo bimbo a chi lo do?
Se lo do alla befana
Se lo tiene una settimana
Se lo do al lupo nero
Se lo tiene un anno intero
Se lo do a lupo bianco
Se lo tiene tanto tanto

Ninna oh ninna oh
A nessuno lo daro.

Lullaby, lullaby, lullaby, ooh
Who will I give this baby to?
If I give her to the kind witch
For a week she will keep her
If I give her to the black wolf
For a whole year he'll keep her
If I give him to the white wolf
For very long he'll keep her
Lullaby, lullaby, lullaby, hmm
To no one I'll give you, my treasure.

As Teresa continued to sing the lullaby over and over, Elisabetta did indeed finally fall asleep. But in between iterations of the lullaby, she heard Teresa quietly weep, "Oh my treasure, I wish I could keep that promise. How will you ever understand? I need to leave you next month. This is not my choice. Papa has decided that I am to go to America."

1911

Elisabetta stood in the center of Piazza Incoronazione, in the same spot where each year she basked in the warmth of the many bonfires to celebrate the end of winter and the Festa di San Giuseppe. All around the small piazza Elisabetta saw a series of three-story apartment buildings, each with shuttered windows, a kaleidoscope of blue, aqua, and orange. The apartments on the second and third floors were surrounded by iron railings and window boxes filled with pretty flowers.

Above the tops of the apartment buildings, she saw the tops of hills surrounding the valley. And looking between the buildings, she saw the steep slopes leading to hills and beyond the hills to the mountains.

On the hills were row upon row of olive trees. The Itrana olives were the pride of this region, bright green in color and speckled with pink, harvested early each year during La Sagra dell'Ulivo— the Olive Festival. The olives produced a fresh and vibrant green olive oil.

Where there were no olive trees, there were fields of brilliant yellow ginestra, a noble flower that suffered from the name "broom" because they were sometimes made into brooms. Across the hills, she could also see thousands of wildflowers, appearing each spring as if by magic, and followed shortly afterwards in June by swarms of fireflies. The alternating fields of ginestra, olives, and wildflowers created beautiful patterns of color across the landscape.

Turning again, she saw a familiar castle, a round tower— the Alligator Tower—with jagged teeth at the top. In medieval times jailers threw the accused off the top and into the moat at the bottom. Leading up to the Alligator Tower was a steep connecting wall with many steps leading up to a rectangular tower, the highest point in the town. From there you could see the four towers out in the countryside that had stood watch over Itri for more than five hundred years, guarding Itri from marauders arriving by ships from the Tyrrhenian Sea or arriving by land through the Via Appia Antica, the ancient Appian Way, running straight through the center of Itri.

Ruins of Roman times were scattered all around town and along the Via Appia Antica. Elisabetta loved to walk along the ancient road, past lines of drying laundry connecting walls that were more than two thousand years old. She would pause in front of the old doorways, lost in thought, imagining the comings and goings through them over the centuries. She loved the ragged stone arches magically held in place by a single capstone. Thousands of pounds of stone held in place by a solitary stone.

Rectangular paving stones were pockmarked by centuries of wear, and laid out in a mosaic of black, gray, and an occasional orange. The stones were all so remarkably symmetrical, seemingly laid in a predetermined pattern and yet simultaneously also somehow unplanned, ordered yet not preordained. At times she thought she could hear dim voices from the stones in the street, sharing their long-forgotten secrets.

On a hot day in July 1911, there were more than dim voices coming from the stones. There were angry voices. The voices rose as more and more townspeople came into the Piazza from one end, and Sardinians—hired to work on the construction of the fifth trunk line of the Rome-Naples railway—poured into the Piazza from the other.

Sweat and arms had been needed for the railroad. A thousand Sardinian workers were recruited, and about five hundred more were working at a construction site a few miles from town. Many had fled Sardinia, eager to avoid the hell of working in the Sulcis mines and desperate for a new life.

Mr. Vincenzo, an *ufficiale anziano* (railway official) at the railroad, was in the middle of it all, towering above everyone on horseback. Something about Mr. Vincenzo had always made

Elisabetta uneasy, even though he was quite an important man in town. He wasn't a bad looking man, but not quite handsome either. But it wasn't his looks; it was his manner. *What exactly is it?* wondered Elisabetta. And then it came to her. He always acted as if *everyone* was a potential threat. He trusted no one. As a result, no one trusted him. Whatever the problem was, he always seemed to make it worse.

As the crowds gathered in the Piazza, and as the Sardinians gathered around his horse and quickly surrounded him, the tension rose. Elisabetta felt shadows—she counted perhaps nine or ten—growing around the Sardinians in the Piazza. They were not shadows of fear or shadows of simple foreboding—she was well acquainted with these—but something far more profound. She shivered as she realized they were shadows of death, and ducked behind a column in front of the church.

Mr. Vincenzo said something—she couldn't quite tell what—that inflamed the Sardinians, and they began screaming curses at him. As tensions rose among the Sardinians, they also rose among her neighbors and her friends in the square—who screamed curses back at them.

Elisabetta breathed a sigh of relief as the *carabiniere* (police) arrived, seemingly out of nowhere, adding even more horse-mounted men and tension to the Piazza. She was astonished when they quickly arrested a Sardinian, a man named Giovanni Cuccuru of Silanus. The yelling and curses grew louder and more fevered until the carabiniere threatened to kill Cuccuru if the protests did not cease and if the Sardinians did not leave the Piazza immediately. The shadows all around the Piazza grew more tense and ominous for Elisabetta until something seemed to break all at once, and the Sardinians left the Piazza.

Over the next few hours, the crowd of townspeople in the Piazza grew. Many of the newcomers brought pitchforks and daggers and guns and sticks. The mayor arrived and councilors and additional carabinieri. Elisabetta *wanted* to leave, and knew she *should* leave, but somehow couldn't.

The noise in the Piazza subsided for a few moments, and Elisabetta noticed that Mr. Vincenzo was once again on his horse and beginning to speak. "Our honor has been challenged! Have we not put up with these foreigners in our midst for long enough?" he yelled over the crowd. "They don't understand our ways! They are taking jobs from Itri men. They don't dress like us or act like us. They are dirty and criminals. They are *sardignoli* (donkeys)."

A huge cheer went up. "We must find these dirty Sardinians and bring them to justice!" someone yelled. The crowd began chanting, "*Uccidili! Uccidili! Uccidili!* (Kill them. Kill them. Kill them.)"

In the middle of them all was Francesco. He was four years older than Elisabetta, and she idolized him. Her papa and Mr. Mancini had even begun to discuss him as a possible husband. Francesco looked so much older than his fourteen years as he screamed with the other men, but he also looked like he was just a boy.

Suddenly they all rode off, gone in gangs in pursuit of the Sardinians, who had fled to the countryside and were in hiding. By the time everything was over, ten Sardinians were dead. Sixty were injured. Many Sardinians who escaped the massacre were arrested on charges of being "quarrelsome." Others were sent back to Sardinia.

Elisabetta—while no fan of the Sardinians herself—had seen a side of Francesco that worried her. A chill went down her spine as she recalled that when Francesco had joined the men in screaming at the Sardinians, shadows of pain—shadows that only she could see—surrounded Francesco as well.

1913

Elisabetta walked up to the big wooden door of the Santissima Annunziata, a church dedicated to the Annunciation. The light streamed in even though the afternoon light was beginning to fade. Some of the candles in the sconces on the sides of the church were lit, adding a bit of an ethereal glow to the church. It was her confirmation day.

Along with the others, she proceeded toward the front of the church and slowly approached the main altar. The black-and-white marble diamond pattern on the floor provided a path for her steps, past the stations of the cross on the side columns, the first seven stations on the right and then continuing with the second seven down the left side to the back of the church.

Elisabetta's eye was drawn off to the side nave, and she recognized the silver statue of Madonna della Città. She loved the annual six-mile procession along the meandering road that wound its way through the Valle d'Itri into the Aurunci Mountains. The Sanctuary of the Madonna was on the peak of Mount Città and from there, you could see in one direction the entire Gaeta peninsula and Ischia. In the other direction you could see Fondi and its coastal lakes and off in the distance, the Pontine Islands. From there, anything seemed possible. She recalled the frequently-told tale of the Madonna della Cività, repeated each year since the fifteenth century.

According to the tale, a deaf and mute shepherd found his lost cow at the base of an oak tree and saw a picture hanging of the Madonna in the tree. The Madonna in the picture smiled at him, and instantly he regained his speech. The sacred painting *Madonna and Child* was said to have been painted by St. Luke the Evangelist. It was believed to have been lost when the Byzantine Emperor Leo III ordered religious persecutions and outlawed sacred images. On the base of the icon, the three letters L.M.P. can be deciphered, even though badly faded. Some people say those initials stand for *Lucas me pinxit*, which is Latin for "Luke painted me." A chapel was built on the spot and in 1492 the Bishop of Gaeta consecrated the first church that was to become the great Sanctuary of Cività.

And from out of nowhere, other words—words from Luke—crashed into her consciousness.

> And in the sixth month the angel Gabriel was sent from God unto a city of Galilee, named Nazareth, to a virgin espoused to a man whose name was Joseph, of the house of David; and the virgin's name was Mary. And the angel came in unto her, and said, Hail, thou that art highly favoured, the Lord is with thee: blessed art thou among women. And when she saw him, she was troubled at his saying, and cast in her mind what manner of salutation this should be. (Luke 1:26-29)

She knew that *that* prophecy for a teenage girl was not hers. It couldn't be hers, and she blushed at the thought. But the nature of this greeting and the "favor" that followed had always preoccupied her. Worried her. What kind of a God issued these sorts of favors? She had always been both drawn to the stories of the saints, and at the same time, terrified by them. We each have some sort of destiny, she thought. What was hers?

As always, Elisabetta's gaze settled upon a statue of the Madonna Addolerata, the Madonna of the Seven Sorrows. The eyes of the Madonna were cast toward the ceiling. The bleeding heart of the Madonna was pierced by seven daggers, each symbolizing a sorrow she would encounter in her life.

The Sorrows of the Madonna both captivated and tormented Elisabetta. The flight into Egypt. The loss of her child, Jesus, for three days. Meeting her son on his way to Calvary. His crucifixion and death. His removal from the cross and finally his burial.

The seventh sorrow—and for Elisabetta the worst—was actually the *first* one revealed to the Madonna. And this was the prophecy of Simeon that she would indeed have a life of sorrows. A life of unanticipated sorrow would be bad enough in itself. But *this* was the truly heartbreaking sorrow: living with the foreknowledge of everything that was to come. She was cursed to know all the sorrows that would follow before any of them had even cast a shadow on her life. The Madonna's worst sorrow of all was knowing her sorrows were inevitable, that they were her lot in life, that these sorrows were her destiny— and she accepted them anyway.

Like the "greeting" from Luke, this was another saintly "greeting" to be avoided, thought Elisabetta. All her life, Elisabetta had received greetings that she would rather have avoided. Mama worried about what she called Elisabetta's moments. Elisabetta couldn't quite explain them. Some of her moments were just that—she would wander off in her mind for a few minutes, forgetting where she was or what she was doing. These were the moments she could tell Mama about. But the others—the dark ones—she kept to herself. They came to her unbidden, and the best way she could describe them was as a shadow or a chill. They were not related to anything actually happening, but were tied to things that *might* happen. During these moments of dread, she was paralyzed, unable to describe exactly what *would* happen, only that she was certain *something* would and that she was helpless to stop it. Even now, standing in the confirmation procession, she could feel the shadows coming. She shook her head to ward them off.

But now she had a protector. She was so thankful that Rita of Cascia had come to her during the confirmation preparations. *Well, she had not actually come to her*, thought Elisabetta, *rather Elisabetta had sought her out*. But then again, maybe Rita *had* come to her. When they were choosing their confirmation names—her namesake for confirmation, the patron saint whose name she would embrace as she received the sacrament—her eye had been drawn to the chapel on the side of the church, a small chapel for Saint Rita, the patron saint of the impossible and of hopeless circumstances.

She didn't know Saint Rita's full story before selecting her as her patron. Once she had selected Saint Rita without any advance thought, she became consumed with her story. This day of her confirmation was also the feast day for Saint Rita. It was surely an omen that she was the right choice.

Saint Rita had wanted to be a nun, but her parents had insisted she marry. The man her parents insisted she marry—Paolo Mancini—was cruel and harsh and ruled their home like a tyrant. She gave birth to two sons, and to protect them she steadfastly responded to her husband's cruelty with kindness. He was murdered because of a rivalry between families, and her sons longed to avenge his death. She then prayed that her sons fail in this revenge, lest they too be condemned to eternal hell as the result of taking a life in anger. God took the sons in response—*He allowed them to be killed*—saving them from eternal damnation.

Such sadness, that a mother would pray for the death of her sons to save them from eternal damnation. *Not really a very satisfactory response to prayer,* Elisabetta thought.

After the death of her husband and sons, Rita was alone. Rita prayed once again that she might become a nun and enter a life of exclusion and isolation and contemplation. But she was rejected again and again because the nuns were worried about the scandal surrounding the death of her husband and sons. The fulfillment of her destiny to become a nun was achieved by agreeing to reconcile her family with her husband's murderers as a condition for joining the convent. Elisabetta marveled at all that it had taken for Rita to achieve her ultimate destiny as a nun.

At times Elisabetta wondered about what it might be like to be a nun, whether this would ultimately be her path. The idea of spending a life in prayer was appealing to her. When she would drift off, deep in her own thoughts, falling into crevices of thought that seemed to engulf her, she wondered whether this was contemplation and prayer or merely an escape. In these moments, she had to consciously pull herself from the crevice, lest she sink deeper and deeper into it.

Thinking back to the fields of yellow that she saw upon entering the church, she suddenly recalled the opening lines to the great poet Giacomo Leopardi's poem to the ginestra, lines that she had had to memorize in school. The words were from the Gospel of San Giovanni: "*E gli uomini volevano oscurità piuttosto che luce*" (And men wanted darkness rather than light).

As she gazed upon her family and friends in the pews, a dull monochrome darkness settled over all of them, especially around the young men. She suddenly sensed her own darkness descending. "*Evitare l'oscurità*" (Avoid the darkness), she prayed to herself.

The Latin of the Mass intruded upon her thoughts and the bishop began the familiar Kýrie, eléison.

Kýrie, eléison. (Lord have mercy)
Kýrie, eléison.
Kýrie, eléison.

But the shadows continued to invade her thoughts. It certainly was a sign of darkness ahead, the advance awareness of trouble for them—death for some—as troubling as the knowledge itself.

Christe, eléison. (Christ Have Mercy)
Christe, eléison.
Christe, eléison.

She began to feel faint and shook her head again to clear the shadows. She prayed to her new guardian Rita for deliverance as the bishop concluded:

Kýrie, eléison.
Kýrie, eléison.
Kýrie, eléison.

The loud questions from the bishop—and his sudden switch back to Italian—broke through her haze and she steadied herself.

"*Rifiuti Satana e tutte le sue opere e tutte le sue vuote promesse?*" (Do you reject Satan and all his works and all his empty promises?)
"*Io voglio.*" (I do.)

"*Credi in Dio Padre onnipotente, creatore di cielo e terra?*" (Do you believe in God the Father almighty, creator of heaven and earth?)
"*Io voglio.*"

"*Credi in Gesù Cristo, il suo unico Figlio, nostro Signore, che nacque dalla Vergine Maria, fu crocifisso, morì e fu sepolto, risuscitato dai morti e ora è seduto alla destra del Padre?*" (Do you believe in Jesus Christ, his only Son, our Lord, who was born of the Virgin Mary, was crucified, died, and was buried, rose from the dead, and is now seated at the right hand of the Father?)
"*Io voglio.*"

"*Credi nello Spirito Santo, il Signore, il donatore di vita, che è venuto sugli apostoli a Pentecoste e oggi ti è dato sacramentalmente in conferma?*" (Do you believe in the Holy Spirit, the Lord, the giver of life, who came upon the apostles at Pentecost and today is given to you sacramentally in confirmation?)
"*Io voglio.*"

"*Credi nella santa chiesa cattolica, nella comunione dei santi, nel perdono dei peccati, nella risurrezione del corpo e nella vita eterna?*" (Do you believe in the holy catholic Church, the communion of saints, the forgiveness of sins, the resurrection of the body, and life everlasting?)

"*Io voglio.*"

"*Questa è la nostra fede Questa è la fede della Chiesa. Siamo orgogliosi di professarlo in Cristo Gesù nostro Signore.*" (This is our faith. This is the faith of the Church. We are proud to profess it in Christ Jesus our Lord.)

Before she knew what was happening, they were all kneeling at the front of the church. The bishop stood over her, making the sign of the cross on her head in chrism. He switched back to Latin:

"*Elisabetta, Rita de Cascia, Et litterae signatae ipsius dona Spiritus sancti.*" (Be sealed with the gifts of the Holy Spirit.)

And the traditional slap, a reminder to be brave: "*Pax tecum.*"

And it was done. She drifted out of the church after the service in a bit of a haze, as usual consumed and a bit overwhelmed by the mysteries of her faith. She was thankful that Rita was now with her and was grateful for her intercession. Without Rita, she feared she might sink beneath the burden of the Sorrows of the Madonna.

The rest of her day was predictable. A meal with the family and friends. And gifts for her. But nothing from her parents. After the guests had left, Mama and Papa pulled her aside.

"Elisabetta, we have something for you." Her mother carefully handed her a beautiful wooden box in the shape of a book. Around the edges on the top of the box was an inlaid design in alternating patterns of red and black, and in the center was a tiny carving. Elisabetta carefully examined the carving. Two small hands hung from a cross.

"The hands symbolize Rita's struggles and her lost sons," said Mama. "May you have her faith but not her troubles." And she crossed herself.

"There is a trick to the box," said Papa. He took the box and showed her how to work it. The center of the box slid out to reveal a compartment big enough for a book. And in the compartment was her own New Testament.

"It is a safe place," Papa whispered. "A place for you."

She was touched at the thought her parents had put into this gift. A commemoration that she would not forget, and that she would never allow to be far from her. A celebration of her confirmation. A place of refuge and safety.

Grateful for the thoughtfulness of her parents and overwhelmed by the day, Elisabetta said a short prayer. *Oh glorious St. Rita, who didst miraculously participate in the sorrowful Passion of our Lord Jesus Christ, obtain for me the grace to suffer with resignation the troubles of this life, and protect me in all my needs. Amen.*

1920

Elisabetta sat in a small ten-foot by ten-foot cabin on the lower bunk of a pair of bunk beds. Between the bunk beds was a steel sink, flanked by two hooks, each containing a towel. Above the sink and connected to it was a water tank, and atop the water tank were two more towels fanned out in an attractive shell pattern. Between the towels was a small mirror.

She looked down at the blanket on which she was sitting and was immediately drawn to the huge circular logo on the blanket. Around the perimeter of the circle were the words White Star Line and in the middle of the circle, a drawing of a flag and the words RMS *Olympic*.

In three short months she would be nineteen years old.

As she sat on the blanket, a flood of memories came to her. She thought about her brother Domenico's marriage to another young Elisabetta in Itri in April. A sister-in-law! How exciting. And with the same name! The huge party afterwards doubled as a wedding celebration and as a bittersweet send-off, because almost immediately after the wedding they had headed to Cherbourg to await passage to America. She had watched Domenico leave once before, likely never to be seen again, only to miraculously return after the war.

Her mind drifted back to other family partings over the years. Her half-brother Michele departed before her earliest memories, leaving for America when she was barely a year old. Sixteen years ago, her sweet sister Teresa boarded the same ship, bound for America. How she ached for her Teresa. She could picture the massive ship and her sad wave as she went aboard. She remembered tears rolling down her cheeks as the ship pulled away from the dock. She had only known Teresa through her letters for the last sixteen years. It was a lifetime ago. And Teresa was married. Married, with three children, and another on the way.

Her sister Adrianna went to the US shortly after Teresa, and then Domenico departed in 1914 from Naples—just a few months before the start of the Great War—aboard the SS *Regina D'Italia*, leaving only Elisabetta, her parents and her sister Maria in Itri. They were a family connected yet now scattered. Distant connections linked by a lifeline of sporadic letters with foreign postmarks and stamps.

Before the Great War began, Papa was glad that Domenico escaped to America to avoid the horrors to come. "It is someone else's war. It is not ours. It will only lead to disaster," he had said. "Thank you, Lord, that Domenico is safe." He cheered the words of the Socialists and the upstart Mussolini: "Down with the war. Down with arms and up with humanity. Stay out of the bourgeois war."

But then just months later, everything had changed. Mussolini asked, "Do you want to be spectators in this great drama? Or do you want to be its fighters?" Many Itri boys dutifully marched off in lockstep in a haze of flags and stolen kisses at train stations and entered the war on the side of the French and the British and the Russians.

By the end of the war, 600,000 Italians were dead, 950,000 were wounded, and 250,000 were crippled for life. The war cost the government more than it spent in the previous fifty years—and Italy had only been in the war for three years. High inflation and high unemployment were everywhere. There was nothing to show for all that bloodshed.

But at least Domenico was safe. Or so Papa thought.

Domenico actually did fight in the war, but for the Americans instead of the Italians and not in Italy but in France—at Baccarat, Vesle, Oise-Asne, and Meuse-Argonne. He was part of the great American offensive that turned the tide of the war—mainly because the Americans still had young men to throw at the fight while the European participants had exhausted their seemingly endless supply. He ended up getting wounded at Meuse-Argonne ten days before the armistice, where more Americans were killed—21,000—than in any other battle of the Great War. After he recovered from his wounds in France, he returned to the United States.

As Papa began to fade, pressure mounted for Domenico to return. His long-distance courtship with Elisabetta Gelfu—Bettina to Domenico—had not been much of a courtship but more of an arrangement since they were separated by the Atlantic. Given Papa's failing vision, Elisabetta was not part of the original plan to return to the US with Dominick and Bettina after the wedding. Elisabetta thought that her future would likely be focused on taking care of her father, but everything changed at the wedding.

Papa announced she was to go to America. And that was that.

So, Domenico not only married Elisabetta Gelfu, but was also charged with bringing both Elisabettas back to America.

That's how Elisabetta ended up on the on the RMS *Olympic*. She stood up from the bunk, walked to the door, and opened it. She looked back at the number on the door, No. 189, and set out to explore the ship.

Elisabetta walked down a short hallway toward the signs that read Ladies' and Gents' Lav. She passed a sign along the way proclaiming that this was indeed the F deck. She walked through the second-class cabins and past what must have been the engines because the noise was deafening and persistent. She continued past some cabins that must have been those of the crew. She wondered at what seemed to be the incongruous sound of barking dogs, and then came upon a sign noting that she was at the dog kennel, full of dogs emigrating to America. *This must be quite a country,* she thought.

And finally, she came to a sign that said Third Class Aft Dining Saloon, and she walked through the door. The saloon was filled with long rectangular tables, seating eight per side. She was surrounded by a babble of languages that she did not understand. She picked up a menu from one of the tables; it was written in multiple languages. Dinner was beef al a mode, lima beans, and boiled potatoes. And something called rice pudding for dessert. Yes, she was a long way from Itri.

"Elisabetta. Elisabetta." Her brother's voice pulled her back from her thoughts. "Are you OK? Always off in some sort of dream, Elisabetta. Sit down and have something to eat."

"Yes, Domenico. I'm fine," she said as she took a seat at the table.

"We were wondering where you had gone off to," laughed Domenico's new wife.

Domenico was ten years older than Elisabetta, and truth be told, her heart was broken when he went to America. She was an infant when Teresa left. But Domenico's departure seemed to put some sort of exclamation point on the dissolution of her family. She was heartbroken, convinced that she would never see him again.

"Are you feeling unwell?" asked Domenico, always solicitous about her well-being. "Are you seasick?" He looked deeply into her eyes to make sure she was paying close attention to what he was about to say. "Elisabetta. Tomorrow we arrive in America. You need to make sure you look healthy when the doctors examine you at the arrival island. And make sure to keep a look out for the famous Douglas Fairbanks and Mary

Pickford. You know they are on this ship somewhere. And while they are in first class and we are in third, I can't help but think that we will see them sometime before we land. Imagine that—the two most famous people in the world are on their honeymoon, and the three of us from Itri are on the same ship, going to the same place: America."

Elisabetta stood up. "I'm fine, Domenico," she said. "I think I will go exploring a bit."

"We will see you later then," said Domenico. "We're going to head back to the compartment to clean up." Their accommodations on the ship were not spacious. Bettina and Domenico and Elisabetta shared a compartment, but they did have their own sink, and meals were provided. However, only two bathtubs served all 700-plus third-class men and women. Elisabetta knew the newlyweds deserved some privacy but nonetheless blushed at the thought. She embraced both and set out.

Deck games such as shuffleboard and quoits and board games such as chess and backgammon were available to second-class passengers. Although there was not much in the way of formal activities for third-class passengers, the aft deck was a popular place to meet, relax, and play deck games. Elisabetta backtracked from the dining room to the stairs. She climbed up two decks.

"It is a beautiful night, is it not?" one of the crew members asked as he came beside her. He was older than most of the other crew members on the *Olympic*. He had kind but sad eyes, eyes that had seen too many things. "This is my last trip on the *Olympic*," he continued. "I have been with the *Olympic* since the beginning, 1910."

Elisabetta watched in silence for a few moments as the huge ship cut through the waves that broke against the hull of the ship again and again. Like all the other passengers, she knew that the *Olympic* was the sister ship of the *Titanic*, and she shivered.

"The *Olympic* was finished first and when we launched, she was the biggest ship in the world," he continued. "The captain was Edward Smith, who later became the captain on the *Titanic*, God rest his soul. The *Olympic* and the *Titanic* were so big that they needed to build a special deep-water dock at Southampton to accommodate them. When we arrived in New York after that first voyage, they opened the ship to thousands of visitors. Ten thousand spectators came to the New York harbor to watch our departure."

As he continued, he turned serious. "We didn't know it then, but the *Olympic* would never again reach the heights that it did after that very first voyage. There has been a shadow following this great ship ever since. Just a few months after our momentous first voyage, after our fifth crossing, we were passing through the Solent, the strait that separates the Isle of Wight from the mainland of England. We were running parallel to the HMS *Hawke*, and as we turned to the starboard, the wide radius of our turn took the commander of the *Hawke* by surprise, and he was unable to take sufficient avoiding action. You must understand that the *Hawke* was a ship specially designed to sink ships by ramming them. The *Hawke* collided with us, tearing two large holes in our hull. The propeller shaft was twisted and some of the watertight compartments were flooded. But no one was injured or killed, and we returned to Southampton under our own power."

"This was certainly a great miracle, sir," replied Elisabetta.

"A miracle, yes. But as you may not yet know—you are so young—miracles are sometimes short lived. And we sow seeds for disaster when we imagine that *we* are the source of these miracles."

"In what way?"

"When the *Olympic* miraculously did not sink, it reinforced what everyone wanted to believe about these great ships. That they were unsinkable. Why bother wasting space for lifeboats if a ship is unsinkable?"

"Eighteen months later, we were returning from New York when we got a distress call from the *Titanic*. We were about nine hundred kilometers away. We set our engines to full power, but when we got to about two hundred kilometers away, we heard from the *Carpathia* that nothing was to be gained by trying to assist the *Titanic*. She was gone. And so, we continued on to Southampton."

They heard the ship's bells, signaling that dinner would begin shortly. "My apologies, Miss. I must go. There was no need for me to go on and on like that. I suppose there is always a part of me that will wonder about those fifteen hundred souls. Especially on this last voyage. It is time for me to leave them behind."

But Elisabetta could not stop thinking about those fifteen hundred souls as she peered into the waves. Those fifteen hundred people also thought they were headed to something new in America, only to encounter disaster. Her worries about the future crowded out dreams about what awaited her in America.

The Madonna's first sorrow—that she would be aware, in advance, of all the sorrows to follow—flooded her with melancholia. Would the Madonna's curse be hers as well? Were the fifteen hundred passengers aware of the shadows that were all around them? Or did they simply stumble into their fate? Even if they glimpsed what was to come, would it have made any difference? Always around the edges of her thoughts were her unspoken suspicions that her own path would not be an easy one.

She eyed the railing of the ship but resisted the impulse to simply cast herself into infinity. She battled the darkness that threatened to engulf her. Everything around her seemed to vibrate, and the sounds around her seemed to alternately echo loudly and painfully through her head or become so quiet that she could barely hear them. She struggled to concentrate, to grasp the chaos that threatened to engulf her. She raised a prayer to Saint Rita and asked for safe passage on her own journey. *Help me to find her way in this new chapter. Help me to leave behind the foreboding that always accompanies my happiness. Give me a sign that dreams lie ahead instead of nightmares.*

As the darkness began to ebb, she sat down on a deck chair. Elisabetta thought about the strange path that had led to this journey to America. At one time, Elisabetta thought she was to be married to the handsome Francesco Mancini. They had been matched by many in their small town since their youth. Papa and Francesco's father, Giuseppe, even spoken of their possible marriage.

Everything happened so quickly once war was declared. Her Francesco Paolo—how the war changed him—was drafted in 1916 into the 1st Engineer Sappers Regiment. They were responsible for building all the trenches and fortifications at the front. The Isonzo northern front was the most dangerous place to be in that hellish war. Isonzo was not just one battle but a continuous back and forth over the same land. There were twelve battles in all before the disaster at the end.

Francesco was shipped north in April 1917, just in time for the worst of it. The tenth of the dozen Isonzo battles in late May had 150,000 Italian casualties. The eleventh battle in the series in August had another 150,000 casualties. And during the final disaster and retreat at Caporetto in October 300,000 soldiers were killed, wounded, or captured. It was a disaster.

The humiliation of the final blow at Caporetto stuck to Francesco like it stuck to many others at the front. *Bad generals!* They reasoned. *They were betrayed! They were stabbed in the back by those at home!* Francesco would tell stories of soldiers at the end refusing to attack in yet another meaningless skirmish. And the carabinieri would materialize seemingly out of nowhere, line up the troops who refused to attack, and shoot every tenth man. Their own countrymen.

When Francesco returned from the war, there was an edge to his unpredictability and a sadness that shadowed him, a sadness that became even more pronounced when he drank. A sadness that turned the medals he received—the Medaglia Commemorativa Della Guerra and the Medaglia Interalleata Della Vittoria—into meaningless trinkets. Trinkets that he threw into the Pontone River on a night when the rages overcame him.

So much changed with the war. A generation of men were gone. All the old rules vanished overnight. There was freedom in the air, but it was a freedom that felt more like chaos than liberty. No one said anything directly—everyone was determined to save face between the families—but the marriage talk stopped, and a shadow grew between Elisabetta and Francesco. Francesco was released from the army in 1920 and then . . .

nothing. Just silence. Never-ending silence from her family, but worst of all from Francesco.

And then barely a month after Francesco's release from the army, Domenico was back, and everything accelerated. Domenico's wedding announcement, the planning for the wedding, and plans for a return to the United States with his new wife paved the way for Papa's announcement: Elisabetta would also be going with Domenico and his new wife. And thus ended any plans with Francesco.

Elisabetta settled into a deck chair, one day away from a new life in America. A life she had neither planned for nor wanted. She was glad to be finally on her great adventure, both eager and fearful for what was to come. Thankfully, Domenico had a place in America. He would help her make the transition. Others from third class were all around her, dressed somewhat formally, as she was. Most of the clothes Elisabetta brought with her for America were, in fact, the clothes on her back.

She dozed in the chair and awoke suddenly to find an attractive fifteen-year-old English boy seated in the chair beside her. He appeared to have been there for some time and was staring intently at her. He was dressed in a simple grey tweed suit. He wore no tie, but a small pocket square added a bit of dash to his appearance. His dark hair parted on one side was longer and more stylish than was the norm in Itri.

"My name is Archie Leach," the boy said. Elisabetta nodded politely, thankful for at least some understanding of English. This boy seemed to possess an extraordinary self-confidence. She responded, simply, "Elisabetta," and blushed.

"I am part of the Bob Pender troupe. We have come from an engagement in London."

Elisabetta did not pick up everything he said, but that did not seem to deter him. She concentrated on understanding what he was saying lest she offend him. Emboldened by her focus, he barged on with a new torrent of words. "We perform pantomimes of fairy stories such as Cinderella, Mother Goose, Puss in Boots, you get the idea. Touring the English provinces with the troupe, I grew to appreciate the fine art of pantomime. No dialogue was used in our act and each day, on a bare stage, we learned not only dancing, tumbling, and stilt-walking under the expert tuition of Mr. Pender, but also how to convey a mood or meaning without words, how to establish communication silently with an audience using the minimum of movement and expression, how best immediately and precisely to effect an emotional response—a laugh or, sometimes, a tear."[1]

Elisabetta nodded politely, catching only bits and pieces.

"I worked so hard to have the confidence of the experienced players. I was determined to once and for all leave my battling parents and be on my own. At each theater I carefully watched the headline artists from the wings. Their timing and confidence! I could not believe it! I decided to imitate everything they did. I thought that I could at least put forward the appearance of being comfortable on stage. And soon I was! The troupe prospered and expanded, and I got a raise to one pound a week pocket money.

---

[1] All of the Archie Leach quotes are drawn directly from Grant, Cary. "Cary Grant Autobiography - The Ultimate Cary Grant Pages," *Archie Leach by Cary Grant*. www.carygrant.net/autobiography/autobiography1.html.

"I got word that Mr. Pender was to choose some members of the troupe to appear in a Charles Dillingham production at the Globe Theater in New York City. Can you believe it? New York City! I decided to attract Mr. Pender's attention by walking the next-to-highest stilts in a graduated line of other stilt walkers, with my head inside a huge papier-mâché mask. On top of the mask was a large, white, limp lady's bonnet with a frill around it. I wore a great calico dress that had frilled collar and cuffs to match the hat. Can you believe my good luck? I was one of eight boys selected to go to New York. So here I am.

"Someday, you will be able to say that you met me, Elisabetta. I will find my destiny in America. The signs are all positive. How else to explain winding up on this beautiful ship? I have even met the famous Douglas Fairbanks and his beautiful wife, Mary Pickford, on the shuffleboard court, of all places. From a tiny English village, from parents who simply could never stop fighting, to London and to a shuffleboard court with two of the most famous people in the world. We live in the most fantastic of times."

While many of the details of this curious monologue were lost on her—she knew she must deepen her knowledge of English immediately upon getting to America—she found herself smiling at his youth, at his optimism. His enthusiasm punctured the rising sense of dread that was her norm when change was imminent. The dread that sorrow would be her lot. An inner sense her life would ultimately be one of sorrow. She prayed for the strength to continue. She prayed for Rita to save her from her own lost causes.

She wondered whether Archie was sent by the Madonna or Rita to give her a message. Although she only understood portions of their conversation, his buoyancy went straight to her heart. How different he was from her Francesco. Where Francesco was dark, this boy was all daylight. Where Francesco was all suspicion, this Archie was all trust.

Oh, the things that could have been. Francesco was different before the massacre of the Sardinians. Before the war. Before the front. But now . . .

And just as suddenly as he appeared, Archie jumped up, bowed slightly at the waist, and said, "I must be going. I am due to meet other members of the troupe for dinner." And with that, he was off.

She thrust her troubling thoughts aside, basking for at least a few moments in the glow of Archie's future. As the evening descended, the wind picked up, and she was cold. She wandered back to their cabin; Domenico and Bettina were already asleep in their bunks.

Seemingly a moment later, Domenico was shaking her awake. "Get up. Get up now, or you will miss it. You will miss her. Hurry. Come up to the Aft Deck as quickly as you can." And he burst out the door.

All their belongings were back in their cases, and the cases were stacked in the middle of the cabin. They were nearing the end of their journey to America. To Egypt and exile? To the Promised Land? To some combination of both?

Elisabetta splashed water on her face, still pondering the ups and downs of the previous evening. She made her way up to the B deck and to the back of the ship. And then she saw it, or rather, her. She had heard of this strange statue by a Frenchman, guarding the entrance to New York City. A giant green goddess in the middle of the harbor, holding a lamp aloft, higher than any building Elisabetta had ever seen. She considered all the hopes and sorrows that had passed before this American Madonna. Elisabetta gazed intently on her face, as usual hopeful for a sign of the future directions her life would take. As she gazed, a vision of Rita came into her mind. Rita, who married Paolo Mancini, a man of strong but undisciplined passions. A man who would give her two sons but would also subject her to the depths of sorrow.

FAMILY TREE 3.0

MY PATERNAL GRANDPARENTS
- Francesco "Frank" Mancini (c. 1900–?)
- Elisabetta "Elizabeth" DeFabritus (c. 1900–?)

THEIR CHILDREN
- Joseph John Mancini (1925–1987)
- Vincent George Mancini (1928–2017)

FRANCESCO'S FAMILY
- Michael Mancini (1884–1934) and Jennie (1889–1972)
  - Luigi Louis Mancini (1910–1926)
  - Josephine Mancini (1912–1992)
  - Joseph Mancini (1914–1920)
  - Eugene Anthony Mancini (1917–1996)

ELISABETTA'S FAMILY
- Michael DeFabritus, half brother (1875–1964) and Rosina Matrullo Sinapi (1877–1953)
  - Angelina DeFabritus (1906–1973)
  - Louis (James) DeFabritus (1912–1997)
  - Marie (Maria) DeFabritus (1914–2015)
  - Jack Gioacchino DeFabritus (1915–1994)
  - Albert Joseph Defabritus (1918–2006)
  - Yolanda DeFabritus (1920–2011)

- Adrianna DeFabritus (1884–1957) and Leonardo Mancini (1876–1968)

- Loreto Mancini (1906–1907)
- Giuseppe Mancini (1908–1908)
- Maria Mancini (1909–1980)
- Edward Mancini (1911–1996)
- Josephine Rose Mancini (1914–1995)
- Molly Amalia Mancini (1915–1993)
- Helen Mancini (1917–2011)
- John Dominic Mancini (1920–1981)

- Theresa DeFabritus (1887–1975) and Frank Ruggiero (1881–1960)
  - Alex Ruggiero (1915–1981)
  - Josephine Ruggiero (1917–2013)
  - Rose Joan Ruggiero (1918–2003)
  - Mafalda Ruggiero (1920–1970)
  - Mary Ruggiero (1923–)

- Dominick DeFabritus (1891–1984) and Elizabeth Gelfu (1894–1984)
  - Marie Frances DeFabritus (1921–)
  - Gloria DeFabritus (1922–)
  - John Thomas DeFabritus (1924–2014)

- Maria Civita DeFabritus (1892–c. 1960)

FOUR

The confirmation that my Italian grandparents arrived in the United States via Ellis Island in the early 1920s gets me wondering about the kind of reception they received. I had heard about discrimination against Italian immigrants and decide this context might be useful in understanding their experiences.

I type "Discrimination against Italian immigrants" into my handy search bar and up pop the first ten of 13.7 million results. Article number one in the search results is the "Grisly Story of America's Worst Lynching" from the History channel:

> Between 1884 and 1924, nearly 300,000 Italian immigrants, most of them Sicilian, moved to New Orleans. The lynching was triggered by the murder of the New Orleans police chief, David Hennessey. As he lay dying, a witness asked him who did it. "Dagoes," he reportedly whispered. Hundreds of Italians were arrested in response, and nine put on trial for the murder.
> After the trial resulted in six non-guilty verdicts and three mistrials, all hell broke loose. "A mob of tens of

thousands of angry men surrounded a New Orleans jail, shouting angry slurs and calling for blood. By the time they were done, 11 men would be dead— shot and mutilated in an act of brutal mob violence that took place in front of a cheering crowd. It was 1891, and the crowd was about to participate in the largest lynching in U.S. history (Erin Blakemore, "The Grisly Story of America's Largest Lynching," History.com, 25 October 2017, The Grisly Story of America's Largest Lynching - HISTORY)

Not exactly a lamp lifted beside the golden door. Lest some of my friends in blue states nod their heads smugly about all of this, here's what the *New York Times* said about the situation:

> These sneaking and cowardly Sicilians, the descendants of bandits and assassins, who have transported to this country the lawless passions, the cut-throat practices, and the oath-bound societies of their native country, are to us a pest without mitigations…These men of the Mafia killed chief Hennessy in circumstances of peculiar atrocity…Lynch law was the only course open to the people of New Orleans to stay the issue of a new license to the Mafia to continue its bloody practices (*New York Times*, 16 March 1891)

Teddy Roosevelt described these lynchings as "a rather good thing." According to CNN's Ed Falco, a local leader named John Parker helped organize the lynch mob. What became of him? Did he go to jail? Did he face disgrace? Not quite.

Parker later went on to be governor of Louisiana. In 1911, he said Italians were "just a little worse than the Negro, being if anything filthier in [their] habits, lawless, and treacherous."

Of course, the accusations of immigrant "otherness" was not a new thing, nor was the discrimination limited to Italians. Just a few years prior to their arrival in the United States, citizens in my grandparents' hometown of Itri were involved in their *own* sins of discrimination – against Sardinians, in 1911. The Sardinians were immigrants to Itri who were eager for work on a railroad construction project.

I am also painfully aware of my own self-satisfied sins of "otherness." I've laughed at insensitive jokes. I've left unchallenged some awful racial slurs. I've made some of my own. Some of this is perhaps traceable to inheriting my father's penchant for conflict avoidance and a desire to fit in. But that's a pretty pathetic excuse, and my own cowardice haunts me.

One of the great things about doing genealogy research is that folks are extraordinarily interested in helping each other solve their puzzles.

Official marriage records from New York City finally reveal the marriage details of my grandparents. They were married on 4 May 1924. Once word gets out that I am looking for the mysterious Frank and Elizabeth, a cousin pops up with a baptismal record from the Mary Help of Christians Church in Manhattan for *her* grandfather, John Thomas DeFabritus. This yields another clue: *The godparents for her grandfather are listed as Frank and Elizabeth.*

Certificate of Baptism

Mary Help of Christians' Church
436–438 East 12th Street
New York, N. Y.

This is to Certify

That _Gioacchino De Fabritis_
Child of _Benedetto_
and _Elisabetta Gelfi_
born in _N. Y. C._
on the _10_ day of _Aug._ 19_24_, was

Baptized

on the _26_ day of _Oct_ 19_24_

— according to the —
Rite of the Roman Catholic Church

by the Rev. _A. Pane_
the Sponsors being _Francesco Mancini_
Elizabeth Mancini

as appears from the Baptismal Register of this Church

Dated _Jan. 12, 1957_ Vol. _1924-25_ Page _33_ No. _322_

Rev. J. Stavaitis Pastor

Nulla adnotatio

Given that my grandparents were married at roughly the same time, I hope that Frank and Elizabeth were also married at Mary Help of Christians and that records at this church might provide some additional clues about my grandparents—like their birth dates, for example, always a useful piece of data in tracking down more data. Mary Help of Christians Church, known for its twin copper-topped bell towers, was built in 1917 and was located at 440 East 12th Street. Unfortunately, it closed in 2007, and after preservationists failed in their efforts, the church was razed in 2013 and is now a lovely building containing overpriced condos.[2] Which doesn't bode well for finding any records.

When Mary Help of Christians closed, the church was incorporated into the nearby Immaculate Conception Church. I hope to strike gold there, and much to my surprise, I do. An extremely helpful person at Immaculate Conception sends me my grandparents' marriage certificate and even provides a handy raised seal version.

---

[2] According to the *New York Times*, at the time of this writing, the condo offers units ranging from one-bedrooms, with an average of 753 square feet, to four-bedroom penthouses, with an average of 2,870 square feet. Most are two-bedrooms. All feature wine refrigerators, washers and dryers and radiant-heat bathroom floors. The eight penthouses have about 11- to 16-foot ceilings and private outdoor space. There are currently 2 three-bedroom units in the building for rent for $16,000 and $19,000 per month. Two units are for sale and can be yours for an average price of $3,937,500.

There on the marriage certificate are my grandparents' birth dates—Francesco, 5 October 1897, and Elisabetta, 25 November 1901. *This is the first time I know their actual birth dates.* The witnesses were Anthony Ruggiere—the brother of Francesco's new sister-in-law, Jennie—and Angelina DeFabritus—the daughter of Elisabetta's half-brother, Michael.

I think about all the Mancini weddings over the years, each one crazier than the one before. Even as the scope of our family has grown, almost everyone makes it a point to be there for weddings. We don't see each other all that often, but there is a connection that persists, which makes the sterile somberness of the memory gap for my father's family even more stark. How did such a connection and history completely skip a generation?

Clearly Francesco and Elisabetta's wedding was a family affair, even though in later years all evidence of this family would disappear—at least to us. But the connection with my long-lost cousin yields something that I had never had before. A photo of my grandparents. A photo of the newlyweds. The only photo that I've ever seen of them.

IMMIGRANT SECRETS

The first official glimpse of my father in the world is in the 1925 census (New York State used to do a mid-cycle census for several years in the late 1800s and early 1900s). In 1925, my father's mother and father had been in the United States for less than five years. Elsewhere on the form, it notes that neither spoke English. They had been married for a year.

I look a bit more closely at this census record to perhaps breathe a bit of life into it and to understand what it might say about life for this new little nuclear family of three, living at 191 East Third Street in Manhattan in the East Village. Looking at Google Maps and exploring a bit, I discover that the current building on the site is the same one that was there in 1925, between Avenue A and Avenue B. The building has six floors and twelve units.

Jane's Exchange is now located on the ground floor. According to Google, it is "a buzzy secondhand shop with a play area & large selection of maternity & kids' clothes, gear and toys." Jane's sounds like a nice business, masking some of the incredible—and painful—stories likely residing deep in the bricks of this building:

> Jane's Exchange is the largest and oldest Children's and Maternity Store in NYC. This unique and child friendly store opened 25 years ago to serve the local East Village community and now serves all five boroughs. We are a grass-roots business and our mission statement includes offering the opportunity to all NYC families to support sustainability in an ecologically and economically challenged time. Put simply, recycling through consignment is a "feel-good" way to help the environment, make shopping for our children more affordable, and support a local business. It's a win-win!! At a time when chain stores and on-line shopping are taking

over, we have a home-grown neighborhood "mom and pop" that offers a wide variety of styles and brands at prices unheard of elsewhere in the city (https://janesexchange.com)

I discover that the census was taken literally weeks after my father was born. The census enumerator—it looks like someone named "Henry Autou"—even directly wrote on the census record for my father, "15 days old." That seems nice and surprisingly personal for a census record. I wonder if my father was born at home or in a hospital.

My grandfather Frank held the unusual occupation of corset cutter. I am sure it was not nearly as glamorous as it sounded and likely had very little to do with Victoria's Secret or even Frederick's of Hollywood.

I try to get a sense of this place, this unusual combination of nationalities, all landing in this one building in the East Village, at a time when it undoubtedly was not as fashionable as it is now. I do some counting of the folks living at 191 East Third Street in 1925. There were 117 people living in the building in 1925. There must have been more flats in 1925 than the current twelve. And likely without aluminum appliances.

The countries of origin for the residents were US (50), Russia (36), Austria (15), Italy (7), Poland (5), Romania (4). Surprisingly, only fifty-one of the residents were listed as aliens. Sixty-six were US citizens. This balance suprises me at first. It seems a lot less melting pot than I always had assumed.

I find myself wondering about this mix of citizens and aliens. And then it dawns on me. Looking back at the sixty-six US citizens living at 191 East Third Street in 1925, I realize that all but six are what are now called (often pejoratively) anchor babies.[3] Frank and Elizabeth were part of a massive chain migration of brothers and sisters who came to the US over a period of two decades, starting with a few people early in the 1900s and then adding to this in ones and twos and threes, all settling in the same area of lower Manhattan.

As I look more closely at the 1925 census record, I realize that Frank's brother Michael, his wife Jennie, and their family lived in the same building as Frank. Perhaps that is why my dad had a certain fondness for an Aunt Jennie, one of the few relatives he ever mentioned.

When I put some of the names of their children from the census record—Louis, Josephine, and Eugene—into Ancestry.com, small green leaves pop up on their records, indicating that Ancestry has found more details about this little family, to whom my grandparents and their new son were inevitably close.

I then come across naturalization papers for Michael dated just a few months after the 1925 census. Jennie eventually became a citizen on 25 June 1951. Sadly, it appears that Michael didn't escape the 1930s. He died in 1934, at only fifty years

---

3   Per Wikipedia, "Anchor baby" is a term (regarded by some as a pejorative) used to refer to a child born to a non-citizen mother in a country that has birthright citizenship which will therefore help the mother and other family members gain legal residency. In the U.S., the term is generally used as a derogatory reference to the supposed role of the child, who automatically qualifies as an American citizen and has the rights guaranteed in the 14th Amendment. The term is also often used in the context of the debate over illegal immigration to the United States.

old. That makes me nervous about my own prospects, since my father died at sixty-two.

On a more positive note, Jennie lived until 1972, Josie until 1992, and Eugene until 1996. Another child, Joseph, was born in 1914, but died in 1920. I wonder if that had something to do with the Spanish flu, which raged during 1919 and 1920. Louis, a.k.a. Luigi, their oldest, was dead less than a year after the 1925 census was taken.

My kids all know their cousins and their aunts and uncles and vice versa. Some of the cousins know each other better than others, as there is over a twenty-year gap from the oldest cousin to the youngest. But at least they *know* of each other.

Now, I will be the first to admit that I'm not very good at figuring out the whole cousins thing. Despite my avowed interest in genealogy and history, when someone says, "they were second cousins, twice removed," I have absolutely no idea what this means. But it's not very complicated with this crowd. Jennie was my father's *aunt,* not some distant and complicated relation. Her presence until 1972 troubles me. As does the fact that Josie and Eugene lived into the 1990s, who would have been *first cousins* of my father. And they all lived in the New York area.

Where were these people? And why no mention *ever* of any of them in our family?

What on earth was that all about?

My quest continues with a journey into the 1930 census.

NAME	RELATION	HOME DATA	PERSONAL DESCRIPTION	EDUCATION
Mancini, Frank	Head	R / $18.00	1/2 M W 32 M 6	no 7/60
— Elizabeth	Wife H		/ W 30 M	no
— Joseph	Son		/ M W 5	no
— Vincent	Son		/ M W 2	no

In 1930, my father was five years old, and the census also documents the arrival of my Uncle Vinnie, born in 1928. They were living at 70 First Avenue in Manhattan, between Fourth and Fifth streets, still on the east side.

Here are a few facts about my grandparents I find in the 1930 census:

- Both responded no to the question of whether they attended school. I'm not sure if they interpreted this as ever or at that time. But both noted that they could read and write.
- Lo and behold, my grandfather seemed to have moved beyond corset cutting. He had grabbed a piece of the American dream and was listed in the census as a fruit stand proprietor.
- They marked that they did not speak English; their language was Italian.
- The value of their home—probably the value of their belongings, since they rented—was $18.00.
- There were five families living at 70 First Avenue. All of them were originally from outside the US. Each family was from a different country: Russia, Poland, Italy, Spain, and

Romania. Only one of the adults was a naturalized citizen, the rest were aliens. Only one family had adults who spoke English.

A variety of other players in my father's family puzzle begin to fall into place via the 1930 census, all living within spitting distance of each other in Manhattan by that point.

In summary:

Elizabeth's side:
- Michael was born in 1875.
- Theresa was born in 1887.
- Dominick was born in 1891.
- Maria was born in 1892.
- Adrianna was born in 1894.

Frank's side:
- Michael and his wife Jennie were born in 1884 and 1889.

Some children and grandchildren of these intrepid immigrants also appear, courtesy of the Ancestry hints.

Almost every single name is unfamiliar to me.

With a name like Mancini people have always assumed that we know something about Italian food. There is even a Mama Mancini's Meatballs, for crying out loud, although I maintain that mine are better. On the occasions when I've been to Italy, the ten extra pounds I regularly put on are testimony to my love of Italian food. It matters not what type. Fish of all types are fine, even anchovies. Pasta, check. Even pappardelle al ragù di cinghiale (ribbon pasta with wild boar sauce) in Tuscany. Cheese, the more fragrant the better, check. You get the idea.

You might think this was the result of many shared family dishes and recipes from my father's youth. But you would be wrong. Truth be told, like the many mystery members of our extended Italian family, we never encountered any of these incredible foods growing up. Well, pizza, but that's more American than just about anything. Ditto for spaghetti with sauce from a jar, back in the days when Ragù only had one variety.

There was one exception: lasagna. I do not know why, but lasagna was my dad's thing. He would start the sauce from paste, adding meat and sausage. The sauce would be bubbling on the stove long before the pasta even made an appearance. Cooking the pasta was itself a bit of an experience. This was before no-cook pasta that you put in a pan dry, only to be "cooked" in the oven when the sauce permeates and softens the hard pasta. The pasta my dad used came out of boiling water. We would leave some of the noodles in the pot, adding olive oil or butter so they wouldn't stick. Then we would spread the rest of them out on the table so they would be ready to be carefully assembled layer by layer—noodle, sauce, sausage, cheese (ricotta, parmesan, and mozzarella)—in the pan.

My father engineered this entire process. I don't even know where my mother was during this. We would assemble for what we knew was coming.

The scraps.

Inevitably, some of the noodles would tear when they were transferred from pot to table to pan. Looking back on it, this was probably done intentionally by my father. If the tear was severe enough, the mangled noodle would go into another pot with extra sauce. There it would sit for mere moments until we would descend upon it, all except my sister, who had some sort of strange and perverse aversion to red sauce and would divert her torn pasta to a bowl with a bit of butter.

I don't even know how much of the finished lasagna we ate, because for us, the scraps were the point of the entire exercise. I'm sure we passed out in a carbohydrate haze long before the actual lasagna appeared.

This was our net experience with Italian cuisine. Like our truncated and hidden Italian family, the only sign of the Italian immigrant experience in our house was that lasagna.

I haven't made lasagna in years. It might be time to do it again.

FIVE

Nè creator nè creatura fu senz' amore
Neither creator nor creature was ever without love.

FRANCESCO AND ELISABETTA, 1920

And now, she was alone.

Once the ship pulled into port, the first- and second-class passengers—Farewell Archie! Farewell Douglas Fairbanks and Mary Pickford!—and the US citizens—Farewell Domenico! Farewell Bettina!—headed one way and the third-class passengers another.

There were hundreds of them left waiting … waiting … waiting for what would come next. Elisabetta asked a crew member in broken English, "How many of us are there waiting here?" He responded, "There were a thousand of you in steerage. All but twenty-five of you are aliens, and you need to wait your turn. You must first go to Ellis Island." Domenico was one of the lucky twenty-five by virtue of his US citizenship, and Bettina as well given the citizenship conferred upon her by marriage.

Elisabetta had heard stories of this Ellis Island from the other passengers. Sometimes, they said, you made it through quickly—maybe three or four hours. Sometimes, passengers were detained for more consideration. And still others were rejected outright and sent back to where they came from.

Domenico said that for most, Ellis Island was the Isle of Hope. But for the unfortunate few who failed the health or legal inspections, it was the Isle of Tears. He had warned her to say as little as possible, to listen closely to the instructions that were given, and to avoid attention.

Finally, a huge double decked ferry arrived, and the first half of them were loaded as tightly as sardines, all dragging their luggage with them, for the short trip. She could see the majestic Green Lady in the harbor and crossed herself for luck. The building ahead was massive; a big red brick structure with arched windows on the first floor and square ones on the second. There were four towers topped with domes and short spires. It looked like a castle.

Once they disembarked, there were lots of pointing fingers and unintelligible commands. They formed a line which stretched all the way from the dock into the baggage room of the main building. Their luggage was tagged, and they were told to leave it; they would get it back later.

Each of them was given an identification tag and an immigration card. On one side, the tag indicated the ship manifest page and line number on which their names appeared and on the back of the card, in ten languages: *When landing at New York, the card is to be pinned to the coat or dress of the passenger in a prominent position.*

At the bottom of the card was a string of tiny numbers from 1 to 14 with the notation "to be punched by the inspecting surgeon." A kind stranger who seemed to have some knowledge of English leaned over and told Elisabetta in Italian, "The tag is to be matched up against the manifest. They will punch the card at each step of the way. Once you get past that, I am told you are in!"

Three abreast they went up a steep flight of stairs. Domenico had warned her of these stairs. "You must not falter on these stairs. The inspectors will not be announced, but they are watching. Watching for signs of weakness. Watching for those they will reject."

At the top of the stairs, they entered a huge room. It was the biggest room Elisabetta had ever seen, probably two hundred feet by one hundred feet. It was called the Great Room. The huge interior space had a high ceiling and the second floor ringed the outside wall and had white railing around it so onlookers could watch those on the first floor below. At the end of the hall there was a huge semicircle window and below that an American flag.

Across the Great Room were row upon row of railings and benches. They threaded the arrivals into organized lines to await their turn with the agents at the front of the hall. All through the hall were inspectors with hole punches or pencils to click off the stages of the process on the numbered card. Strangely, some also went about with chalk, going from person to person while they waited, looking for signs of weakness, occasionally chalking a single letter on someone and yanking them out of line.

"These letters," whispered Elisabetta to the kind stranger behind her. "What do they mean?"

"They are marked for weakness. The X means they fear that person might be feeble-minded. The P means they have seen you breathing hard and fear for your lungs. The C means they see red in your eyes and fear an eye disease. I am not sure about the other symbols."

Elisabetta could feel the room begin to fall away from her at this news and struggled to look straight ahead. She could feel—at least she thought she could feel—a thousand eyes looking at her, probing for her secret weaknesses. She said a silent prayer:

> *Oh glorious St. Rita, who didst miraculously participate in the sorrowful Passion of our Lord Jesus Christ, obtain for me the grace to suffer with resignation the troubles of this life, and protect me in all my needs. Amen.*

She pushed forward, one step after the other. Occasionally when the line would stall, she would sit down on the benches that ran along the rails.

I have been in this room for hours, she thought.

Just survive. Don't stand out. Don't be pulled from line.

The noise in the room was deafening and the number of languages uncountable. Every so often, strings of Italian, voices of home, reached her ears through the cacophony.

When will this journey end? All this way, so much confusion.

She thought back to her time on the deck of the ship, at the inviting waves below, and wondered whether she had been right in resisting the temptation to leap. One by one, the passengers were called forward to speak with a uniformed inspector seated on a tall stool behind a high desk. Interpreters helped the immigrants communicate. After an eternity, she arrived at the front of the queue. And the questions began. One after the other in rapid succession:

> *Where were you born?*
> *Are you married?*

What is your occupation?
Have you ever been convicted of a crime?
How much money do you have?
What is your destination?

Oh, for a sign of kindness or encouragement from this man. The inspector marked her identity card and motioned for her to pass.

She moved to the top of another staircase at the other end of the Great Hall. This staircase had three lanes. People who were traveling west or south walked down the right side of the staircase. Those going to New York City or to the north walked down the left side.

When the official at the top of the stairs saw the mark on her card, she was directed to the center aisle. She found an interpreter. "What is the problem? I am supposed to go to the left, to the stairs for New York City, to meet my brother Domenico."

"There is a problem. The marks on the card indicate there is a problem that needs to be reviewed. You must go down the middle stairway."

As she slowly descended the stairway, her knees grew weaker at each step. She fought off the shadows that seemed intent on engulfing her. At the bottom, she was directed to another set of stairs. This time she was headed back up again to the third floor, women on one side, men on the other. An interpreter informed her once again that there was a problem with her card. She would need to stay in a room filled with beds until things were sorted out. When she asked, "How long?" the interpreter shrugged his shoulders.

What would Domenico do? she asked herself. *What would he think? How would he find her? Their plan was to reunite today after she passed through the island. What now?*

She lay down on the bed and began to weep and was soon asleep.

1924

The flash of a camera startled Elizabeth out of one of her moods, a trance in which she would vanish into herself and her thoughts. For a moment she had no idea where she was. She thought for a passing moment she was back in the dormitory on Ellis Island, from which she thought there was no exit. She had remained in a panic on Ellis Island overnight until Domenico rescued her by showing up and asking questions. A hearing was held, and "they" realized that a mistake had been made. Thank goodness Domenico, an American citizen with understanding of these processes, had been waiting on the other side.

Out of the corner of her eye she caught a glimpse of herself in a large mirror on the other side of the room. And the handsome—although not terribly tall—man that was standing next to her. The path to her wedding to Francesco had not been a straight one. She said a prayer for her many blessings.

No sooner had she departed for America—leaving Francesco and the long-planned marriage behind—than new wheels were set in motion, changes that would determine the path of her life. Every day she would roam the streets around their apartment, baffled by the languages and the loudness of everything. It was so unlike Itri. She missed the yellow ginestra and the olive trees and the wildflowers of home. She was not sure exactly what she was supposed to do now that she was here. She prayed for some sort of sign. Desperate for something—anything—to grab on to. Desperate for a sign that this was indeed the path for which she was destined. Desperate to someday love again and be loved.

Then the letter from Francesco had arrived. He must have mailed it shortly after she left. The letter had arrived in America just a few weeks after she did, at a time when she was so homesick for Itri that she could barely stand it. Domenico tried to hide Francesco's letter from her. But she found it, and it opened a flood of feelings.

> My Dearest Elisabetta:
> I now realize the dreadful mistake I have made. This will not be a long letter, because you know I am not a man of many words.
> But for whatever pains I have caused you—for the life that we might have had that I now have thrown away—I must now suffer.
> My thoughts are scattered, and I fear that my nerves will never be the same. The one certainty in my life has always been you. And now you are gone. But you will always have my heart.
> Francesco Paolo.

Elisabetta clung to his letter like a life preserver against the flood of sorrows that she feared lay ahead of her. After all, she was now almost past the age of marrying. The war had depleted the supply of young men and certainly reduced the likelihood that she would have anything but a life alone.

The more Domenico told her that Francesco was not for her, the more Domenico reminded her of Papa, and the more she grew fearful that a life without Francesco would indeed be one of sorrow. She was, after all, not a great beauty. And to be a woman without a man in this strange country was a recipe for sadness.

Ahh, Francesco.

She prayed each night for relief from her uncertainty, for a sign to help her know what she was to do. She longed for a sign to point her in a direction, any direction. And all the while, the cacophony of questioning voices in her own mind grew louder. She prayed to Rita, her adopted namesake and patron saint of all lost causes.

During the day, Elisabetta had walked the crowded streets of lower Manhattan, trying to find meaning in the confusion of her life. She missed the warm sun and the mountains of Itri. In Manhattan there were just buildings, huge buildings, that crowded out the light and the sun. While her English improved quickly, all the English voices still struck a dissonant chord that seemed to constantly assault her ears.

And then he was there.

As she thought back to that day in May 1921 when Francesco had appeared at her door, she realized that his appearance was what she was waiting for, what she longed for.

A sign.

Francesco quickly got a job as a corset cutter. He had worked like a man possessed, determined to prove to anyone who might have doubted that they were wrong about him. That they all were wrong.

Throughout 1922, letters from Itri had reported that Papa's blindness and dementia were becoming worse and worse. Domenico became the voice of authority in the family. And when Papa died in 1923, it was a foregone conclusion that Domenico was the patriarch. As the days passed into weeks and then months, Domenico had begun to soften; perhaps Francesco was indeed the man for his sister.

And a wedding was planned. First, they headed to the court to get the license. They encountered a confusing array of English signs and English speakers with little patience for any language other than English. Thank goodness her cousin Angelina—a long time veteran of American processes—was there along with Jennie's brother Anthony.

Elisabetta gazed in astonishment at the ornate lace of her wedding dress, the beautiful veil on her head, and the huge bouquet of roses in her hand. Francesco looked dashing in an elegant tuxedo, complete with a cummerbund with sparkling buttons, high collar shirt, and white bow tie.

In the absence of her father, Domenico and Bettina handled all the arrangements: the flowers, the reception, and the wedding dinner. As was the custom back in Italy, her family gathered before the wedding at Dominico and Bettina's, while Francesco and the Mancinis gathered at Michael and Jennie's. From there, each group headed over to the Mary Help of Christians Church. As Elisabetta approached the pretty white church with the two-small, green-topped towers and three arched doorways—just like the Santissima Annunziata—she thought about how far she had come. All the worries about Francesco were now behind her.

She walked down the center aisle with Domenico, past the multiple arched marble pillars, and past the Stations of the Cross on the side aisle. Her path was now clear.

Later that night, Elisabetta quietly got up, walked softly into the other room, and retrieved her precious confirmation wooden box. She made the sign of the cross on the top of the box and carefully opened it. She looked down at all the precious things she had placed there since her confirmation: fragments of her life, precious things to remind her that perhaps sorrow was not to be her destiny, that some other future awaited. She placed a rose from her wedding bouquet in the New Testament, slowly closed the box, and put it away for safekeeping.

She recalled their signatures—Francesco and Elisabetta—on the marriage license. She resolved that the past would not stand in her way. She resolved to exorcise the demons in her head and commit to this new life. She resolved that this was no longer the story of Francesco and Elisabetta. It was the story of Frank and Elizabeth.

Farewell, Madonna Addolerata. Farewell, Rita.

Freedom.

1925

Elizabeth looked down at the tiny baby in her arms, stunned to realize that he was, in fact, hers. She wondered if she had finally escaped the sorrow that seemed to foreshadow everything in her life. As she looked at this baby, she could see nothing but love. Perhaps he was a cure to the troubling shadows that always disrupted her joy, the shadows that appeared so unexpectedly and with so little warning.

She had such hopes for this tiny one. She looked deeply into his dark eyes, realizing that perhaps in those eyes lay the answer to the demons who troubled her, the sense of pending doom that she could never quite escape.

The table was set with the foods she loved, foods from home: pasta e fagioli, polenta with sausage ragù, risotto with porcini mushrooms, and linguine with asparagus. Someone even managed to get some delicious Marzolino cheese. She so loved this special cheese from Itri.

"Well," Frank said, clearing his throat. Elizabeth looked around to realize that she was not in fact alone in a cocoon of soft ethereal light with her new son. She was in their flat in the East Village on Third Avenue—with Frank.

Frank was everything he promised when he had first talked his way back into her life. Papa and everyone else were so wrong about him. She thought back to her first doubts about him, when he seemed so full of hate at the thought of those Sardinians threatening to take what belonged to true Italians like himself. She thought of when he returned from the War, not injured, but truly broken, a shell of the man he once was. And then she recalled the crushing news that there would not be a wedding after all but a ticket to America.

But Frank persisted. He wrote to her. He came to the US. Little by little, brick by brick, he had dismantled the wall between them. He found work as a corset cutter—hard work, but regular work with a good wage at the Nemo Corset Company—and they married.

She looked around their small apartment. There were just two rooms, each about twelve feet by fifteen feet. They had running water in the apartment and didn't need to go down to a well. There was much conversation in their building that soon the outdoor outhouses would be replaced by bathrooms on each hall and perhaps even showers. She and Frank slept on a folding bed in the front room. Each morning they would carefully fold the bed so there would be more room.

Once Frank went off to work, Elizabeth would set to work in the kitchen and spent most of her day there. Twice each week she washed their clothes, scrubbing them in the sink, back and forth, back and forth across the washboard, wringing them until her hands ached and then hanging them to dry on the line in back of the apartment. She marveled at the strange cacophony of Italian and Russian and Polish and German—and yes, English—that flew out from the windows of their building. What a place they had come to.

Even through April and May—when she felt she was as big as a horse—she would work every day to scrub the apartment. Their apartment was one of the few within the building with the fancy new linoleum—such elaborate patterns, just like a rug. She would get down on her hands and knees to make sure that she got everything clean.

She struggled to stretch Frank's paycheck from the corset company. With no garden, food was so expensive. How she missed her garden in Itri and the hours spent planting and weeding and harvesting, all in the warm air. When she did leave the apartment, it was usually to roam the neighborhood to find fruits and vegetables and flour to make pasta and bread. But Sundays—oh Sundays—they would have meat with their dinner.

A knock on the door disrupted her thoughts. Frank opened the door a crack and in came a rush of people, led by Frank's brother Michael and his wife, Jennie. She knew that Jennie would love this tiny baby like one of her own and would watch out for him. Close on their heels followed their children, Louis, Josie, and Eugene. Louis was fourteen and thought he was ready to take on the world. His younger sister Josie was twelve, and largely still in awe of her older brother. Eugene had just turned eight. Following right behind them was Jennie's mother, Lucy, and Jennie's younger brother, Anthony, both of whom also shared their small apartment. Lucy had helped her during those times when she so missed her own mother. She had also—unbeknownst to Frank—slipped her the odd dollar or two when the money was just too thin. She felt so blessed to have them all—an entirely new family—living in the same building.

Elisabeth was happy. The old cloud around Frank was gone, and the cloud that seemed to follow *her* as well. She looked at Frank and realized that he was in fact not just an "arrangement." He was the father of her beautiful son, a son who looked up at her with the eyes of the future. She hummed an old lullaby from home while gently rocking the precious baby in her arms:

Ninna nanna, ninna oh
Questo bimbo a chi lo do?
Ninna oh ninna oh
A nessuno lo daro.

Lullaby, lullaby, lullaby, oh
To no one I'll give you, my treasure.

> Lullaby, lullaby, lullaby, oh
> Who will I give this baby to?

Frank interrupted her reflections. "I think it is time we name him," he said.

Elizabeth handed her son to his godmother, her niece Angelina—daughter of her own half-brother, Michael, who had left Itri so many years ago. Frank's brother Michael and Elizabeth's half-brother Michael had each been the first in their families to stake a claim in America. The baby's godfather, Anthony, Jennie's brother, exclaimed, "Yes, it is time for us to name this little one."

Frank stood up and began to speak. "I wish to name him Giuseppe, or Joseph in the eyes of the Americans, in celebration of my father. And to honor the great Garibaldi, who united Italy. And I pray the Lord shall grant me another son!"

Elizabeth realized that Frank was on the verge of one of his great speeches. He was a man of so much passion that he would sometimes run off into excess. But he soon regained his composure. He continued enthusiastically but without a hint of the tensions that sometimes seemed to follow quickly on the heels of his passions.

"And for the middle name, I propose Giovanni—God is gracious. God has shown favor." Knowing that the naming of a son was something that traditionally fell to the father, Elizabeth said nothing. But truth be told, she had known from the moment she saw him that this baby would be called Joseph John. *God is gracious and good,* she thought, *and His plans for me are not yet finished.*

"This," Anthony pronounced, "is a great moment. I am an uncle!" Everyone laughed. Frank's brother Michael reached over to take the baby from Angelina. "Yes, it is a great moment but not for you. This is a great moment for the Mancinis in America. My younger brother is a father." Frank beamed with pride, always an easy target for both his older brother's ire and praise. Jennie realized that she should perhaps take control before these two Mancini brothers went over the edge, and she reached over to take the baby.

Jennie looked deeply into the baby's eyes, and she knew that this nephew would indeed have a special place in her heart. She loved all of them—her own children and her nieces and nephews—but this one would be special. How fortunate they were to live next door.

Josie could barely contain herself. She was the perfect age to dote on a baby. Eugene was largely oblivious to the charms of a baby, realizing that there was now a younger challenger to everyone's affections. Louis quietly looked on, seemingly lost in some private reflection of his own, patiently waiting for his turn to hold the baby.

When Louis' turn came, Elizabeth felt a strange chill come over her, a familiar sense of foreboding that she simply could not explain. As she looked closely at Louis and Joseph John, a shadow passed, and she knew that one would not survive the year. She said nothing but just silently prayed to the Madonna. "*Oh Madonna Addolerata, I pray to you as a mother. Let this shadow pass. Let both these boys grow into men, for the world needs them.*"

And the shadow did pass. Her joy returned and she was allowed a moment of pure and uncharacteristic joy. "*Oh Madonna, thank you for the gift of my son.*"

SIX

Just as I think our family's story was unknown but pretty much a typical immigrant experience, I come across the 1940 census. Most people don't realize that census data is sealed for seventy-two years.[4]

The good news (sort of) is that Frank and Elizabeth were alive in 1940. So much for the "They died in the 1930s" story. And now the bad news.

Frank was at the Rockland State Hospital in New York. To make matters worse, the Rockland State Hospital is a psychiatric hospital. It was known at the time as the Rockland *Insane* Asylum. He's listed in the 1940 census as an inmate.

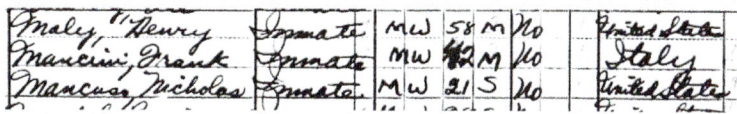

---

4 The U.S. government will not release personally identifiable information about an individual to any other individual or agency until 72 years after it was collected for the decennial census. This "72-Year Rule" (92 Stat. 915; Public Law 95-416; 5 October 1978) restricts access to decennial census records to all but the individual named on the record or their legal heir. After 72 years, the records are released to the public by the National Archives and Records Administration. In accordance with the 72-Year Rule, the National Archives released the 1930 records in April 2002 and most recently, the 1940 records were released 2 April 2012.

The state of New York is notoriously obstinate about the release of health records—even to direct relatives. I went through many New York State health system dead-ends trying to find out what had happened to my grandparents.

During this journey, I came across a terrific book, *Annie's Ghost*, by former *Washington Post* writer Steve Luxenberg. In it he describes his somewhat similar journey across the psychiatric commitment landscape. When his mother died, Luxenberg discovered he'd had an aunt, warehoused for many years in a Detroit mental hospital. Why hadn't he and his siblings been told? He launched an investigation into his aunt's history, which led to an investigation into the asylum system itself. Each discovery raised more questions.

I contacted Steve about my health record dead ends to see if he had any ideas on how to proceed. He suggested that I go down the path of finding the original commitment papers. He told me that *legal* documents have a different set of privacy restrictions associated with them than do *health* documents.

So that's what I decided to do.

I call up the court archives in Manhattan and tell the helpful guy who answers the phone that I am looking for commitment records from back in the 1930s. I don't really expect much after all the dead ends.

"Wait just a second,' he says. "Let me see if I have a card for that." A card? Hmm, my digital prejudices kicked in.

"Yes, I have one right here for Frank Mancini, 1932."

I couldn't believe it. "Say what? That easy? Well, where are these records?"

"Here's the number for the court records room. The file you should ask for is 34118/1932."

Well, I'll be damned.

When I call the records room, another very helpful person says they will request the records, and they will be available in room 103B in three days.

The Supreme Court Building, originally known as the New York County Courthouse, is a New York landmark. It has big columns and a wide staircase leading up to the main doors. In New York fashion, the staircase is compromised by fencing, limiting access to only a two-person spread so that no one can sit—or sleep—on the steps.

As I climb those steps, I realize I am walking onto a movie set. Many films and television shows were shot at the New York County Courthouse, including *Miracle on 34th Street* (1947), *12 Angry Men* (1957), *The Godfather* (1972), *Wall Street* (1987), *Goodfellas* (1990), and a host of others. New York must not have gotten paid very much for these location shots, though, because the interior of the building is … well, let's just say it's austere. Or maybe it's just been untouched since the building's opening in 1927. Not to be overly dramatic, but I can almost feel the ghosts of Frank and Elizabeth hovering in the huge hexagonal foyer like a pair of Harry Potter dementors.

After searching the first floor for room 103B, I ask a security guard for directions. Fulfilling all the records management stereotypes out there he tells me, "They're in the basement."

Once I arrive at 103B, I fill out some additional paperwork and show my email to a fellow in a New York Yankees T-shirt, proving to him that someone on the staff has promised that the records are in fact there. I resist the impulse to make disparaging comments about the Yankees, reflecting upon the fact that a) my father (and truth be told *me* for my first twenty years) was a New York Yankees fan, and b) I need this guy to get me my records.

A few moments later an accordion file folder is in my hand containing the records for a 16 August 1932, court proceeding. As I contemplate opening the file to find out how and why my grandfather began his journey to Rockland, I pause and wonder whether I really want to do this. Do I really want to bring these ghosts to life? Are they better left asleep? Why had it all been kept a secret for so long? What is the path to best honor my father? Is it to free the ghosts of the past from their prisons, or is it better to keep them chained? I wonder what exactly I am trying to accomplish with all of this.

I realize there is no turning back at that point. Once I open the folder, I will know *something*. I will have some clue about the secrets that my father kept for his entire life.

Even with some clues that the contents of the folder will be unpleasant, the front of the document is still a bit jarring. The document is labeled Certificate of Lunacy. No mincing words there. And Frank's legal status is Indigent.

DEPARTMENT OF MENTAL HYGIENE

PETITION, CERTIFICATE OF LUNACY

AND

ORDERS

IN THE CASE

OF

MANCINI, Frank

Resident 70 First ave.

County New York

Date of Order of Commitment

Aug 16, 1932

Institution Rockland State Hospital

Date of Admission Aug 17, 1932

No. of Case Book , Page

No. for Year 158

Consecutive No. 4185

Identification No.

Legal Status (*State whether indigent, public or private*) Indigent

Frank was certified insane by two Bellevue doctors, Carter N. Colbert and Lauretta Bender. He was then committed to the Rockland Insane Asylum. The diagnosis was dementia praecox, the diagnosis for about half the inmates at asylums of the time. It was a catch-all precursor to the diagnosis of schizophrenia.

The *only* mention any of my siblings can remember my father making about *his* father comes from my brother Joe:

> One time I went out, and I drank too much. I came home and I threw up. The next morning, we were down in the family room. Dad came down, and he looked in the room said, okay, who was it? John immediately pointed to me. And all I remember him saying was, "I remember my father coming home and throwing up in the sink."
>
> And that could be the only thing in my entire life I ever heard him say about his parents.

SEVEN

La speranza e l'ultima a morire.
Hope is the last thing to die.

FRANK AND ELIZABETH, 1931

When Joseph heard the yelling, he knew he needed to hide. He grabbed Vinnie by the arm and headed as far from the yelling as he could, which in their tiny apartment, was not far.

They huddled behind the bed and waited for the storm to subside.

"Be very quiet, Vinnie," he said, although at only three years of age, there was little chance that Vinnie would understand. But he seemed to understand the urgency in Joseph's voice, the plea for calm.

"We must imagine we're invisible," he whispered to Vinnie. "If we are invisible and very quiet, maybe he will stop."

He was Papa. Joseph knew if they waited long enough and if they were good enough and if they were quiet enough, eventually Papa would stop.

Why was he like this? Joseph thought. *He wasn't always like this. What have we done to make him like this?*

The tiny boys huddled together even closer as the yelling intensified and the hitting began. "Sh, sh, sh," he whispered to Vinnie.

Scream. Hit. Scream. Hit. Crying.

And just as suddenly as it had begun, it was over. And quiet.

"It's safe now," he told Vinnie.

1931

The descent came so quickly that Elizabeth had not seen it coming.

At first Frank only took minor offense to what he interpreted as slights. Elizabeth would try to talk him through these slights and get him to understand that the comments were never meant to cause harm. Or if they did have an edge to them, he should just ignore them.

So many times, smug storekeepers would make fun of his broken English. Or to be more accurate, his Italian punctuated by a few words of English because Frank had never been very patient with learning English. Each insult led to yet another store being put on Frank's list. "We are done with that place. You are not to shop there ever again," he'd say. And she knew that this was not a conversation; it was a pronouncement.

Even the most cursory comment would set him off, into a rage that he managed to only keep under control until he got home. Once home, he would drink glass after glass of wine.

He would long for his life back in Itri, drinking until he could speak no longer and would simply fall asleep.

Up and down, up and down Frank's moods would go. Elizabeth lived for the highs and suffered through the depths. When he was younger it was mostly highs. That was the Frank—the Francesco—with whom she had fallen in love. He had always had this sense that he was destined to do great things, that he possessed qualities that other men did not. He had an enthusiasm at these times that carried along everything and everyone in its wake, including her.

He had opened the fruit stand with his brother during one of these peaks, and it forestalled his descents for a time. He was proud to be part of something he owned. As usual, he was eager to be a success. But he couldn't realize that simply wishing it so would not make it happen.

As the Great Depression deepened—both the country's and his—he simply stopped going to work. He would stay in the apartment, claiming some ailment or another. He was unable to get out the door. He would stare at the wall, longing for some miracle to occur, but he was not willing—or able—to make it happen. He would be lost in his own thoughts, occasionally mumbling to the wall.

For hours on end, Frank simply stopped talking. Elizabeth missed his voice. When he did talk, it was in a flat, unfocused tone. "I feel like my voice is swallowed up, deep in my throat," he said. She was not sure what to make of this. "When I walk across the room, it is as if my feet are falling through the floor. Each step is like a step off the ledge."

The money got tighter and tighter. Elizabeth was worried how they would stay in the apartment. They had missed the rent a few times, but during the times when Frank's shadow would lift, he would work like a crazy man and make good on the back rent. The creepy landlord would make comments to her as she would come and go, comments that no man should be able to make to a married woman, comments that she could not repeat to Frank, for they would surely push him over the edge.

At the end of 1931, Frank's cycles worsened. As his highs got higher and his depths sank lower, Elizabeth grew increasingly afraid, uncertain what to do. In the worst moments, he would blame her for his pain. "If it wasn't for you, we would not be in this place. Why did you have to leave Itri and have me chase you like some puppy here to America? To this country where we are treated like dirty Sardinians? To this place where we are surrounded by your family, all of whom look down on me?"

Of course, she could have simply left him. Her family would have most certainly taken her in, but that would demonstrate that they had been right about Frank all along. She did not think she could survive it. She did not want to go scurrying back to them, crowding their apartments, living like a common peasant.

She ended up forcing Frank to go to work. She threatened to go to the police and tell them he was refusing to support them. "Frank, you must go," she said. "Your brother is waiting for you at the fruit stand."

"Do not tell me what to do. I am feeling sick in the stomach today. No one can expect me to go to work under such conditions."

Elizabeth knew how the conversation would end, and she was determined that today it would not end the way it always did. "Frank, the rent is overdue by two months. You must go."

"And if I don't, what are you going to do? Call the police again? On a sick husband? And where will you be then if I am in jail and cannot earn a living. Stupid woman, tend to the children and make my breakfast."

She decided that she had heard enough. "Today, there will be no breakfast unless you promise me that you will go to work," she pleaded.

He struck her face hard with the back of his hand. She staggered back. "You will do as I say," he bellowed.

In their small apartment, Joseph and Vincent saw and heard all of this. At three years old, Vincent was too young to understand most of it. At six, Joseph did not truly understand, but he did know that something was horribly wrong. There was no place to hide in their small rooms. Joseph cowered in the corner, holding Vincent close to him, afraid that if he came forward, he would also feel his father's wrath.

Frank looked from face to face, unsure of what had come over him. And just as quickly as it had started, it ended, and he stormed out the door.

But the shadows were growing.

1932

When does sorrow become inevitable rather than just a possibility?

When does the tipping point occur?

When do you just need to walk away?

These were the questions that weighed on Elizabeth's mind as she sat alone in their apartment, pondering everything that had happened.

When Frank refused to go to work and they had run out of money, she had taken him to Family Court. He begged for forgiveness and promised things would change. And they would for a little while, but then it would happen again. And the humiliating cycle would repeat itself as the highs became higher and the lows became lower. She even had him arrested, and they kept him in jail for ten days.

He had always had an overwhelming appetite for sex, more than she could handle. When he was drinking, he would boast of all the women—countless women during the war—that he had long before her. But she discovered in the end that there were worse things than his boasting.

He suddenly became impotent and began to accuse her of having affairs. With the owner of the Ries and Eichengreen clothing store in their building at number 70. With the clerk in the furniture store at number 68. And worst of all, with the landlord in their building, Mr. Vivino.

The tirades were long and loud and horrible. He yelled that she was trying to take away his position as the father of the family. That the father was the head of the family and that her role was to obey. That *he* was the head of the family. A tirade of curses would rain down from their apartment: "Porca puttana! Stronza! Baldracca! Zoccola!" They were audible to anyone passing by.

She still tried to counter what now seemed inevitable. Despite all evidence to the contrary, despite the visions of Madonna and Rita that had long previewed her sorrow, she lived in her own universe of unrealistic hopes. But as the shadows on Frank's mind became more than he could handle, and as the inner voices in his mind crowded out the real ones, Elizabeth began to despair.

That August day in 1932 was predetermined to happen. She sensed it always was destined to happen, although the day had started out like any other.

They had had their usual argument. She urged him to go to work in the fruit stand, and he refused to leave the apartment. Finally, she convinced him to go. She thought he went to work, but he went to some back-alley bootlegger friend to drown his sorrows and dull his pain.

She felt him coming up the stairs of the apartment more than she heard him. She had developed a sixth sense when it came to Frank and his moods, and that day she knew there would be trouble. The torrent, mostly in Italian, started as soon as he slammed through the door.

"When did he leave?" he stormed. "How long ago was he here? I can smell him. I know he was here. Where is that bastard? I know you two have been plotting and scheming against me. Plotting to take my boys away—MY BOYS!—and poison me! Don't lie to me, you *porca puttana*! Admit it! Now! Admit in the presence of your sons that you are a lying whore, scheming away with that landlord to kill me!"

Over the past six months, as he became increasingly excitable and forgetful and more and more unpredictable in his moods, he had developed the idea that Elizabeth was trying to poison him. He would carefully smell every food that was put in front of him.

"You think I am stupid! You think I don't know. But I know of these things! You forget that I knew of these things in the war. The smell of pineapples and pepper would be in the air, and then the chlorine would hit, eating out your lungs. And the coughing and the vomiting and the blindness. I can smell it everywhere! I can smell it in the food you make for me! I can smell it on your clothes and on the clothes of that bastard Vivino. Elisabetta, how could you do this to me? I've given up everything for you. I was to be a great man! A great man!"

Suddenly the door opened. Mr. Danilewicz from across the hall poked his head in. Mr. Danilewicz spoke mostly Polish, and Frank was screaming mostly in Italian, but it was evident that something unusual was going on. Everyone in the building typically minded their own business, particularly if it was just a wife being taught a lesson, but this was too much.

"Elizabeth, are you alright?" he asked, using the few bits of English he knew, assuming that Frank would not understand.

"What are you saying, you Polish scum? Don't you talk over me! Are you part of this too? I've seen you and that Vivino talking in the hallways. Have you also been laughing at me, hiding your poisons in that disgusting Polish food? Is my whore wife also spreading her legs for you, too? She won't give me the slightest attention, but she will spread them for everyone else!"

Elizabeth worried that if she said anything, things would quickly move to the next level of danger. She was not so much worried for herself, but she had realized months ago that she was the only one who could possibly protect Joseph and Vincent. She prayed every day that something would rescue them from the disastrous path they were currently on, one that she was afraid could only end in destruction.

She cast a panicked glance at Joseph and Vincent, who were huddled in the corner. She then looked directly at Danilewicz, willing him with her eyes to understand that *now* was the time that they had talked about for the past six months. Now was the time to get Frank's brother Michael and get Frank out of there. Thank God they had discussed a plan for when things would finally go over the edge. Even if she needed to have him arrested or admitted into Bellevue, she needed him out of the apartment.

Danilewicz gave her an almost imperceptible nod and she knew. Michael was coming. She just needed to keep things under control until he got there. Now was the time to talk Frank down from wherever he was. "Francesco," she began softly. At the mention of his name—his real name—the spikes of anger and rage began to drain out of him, almost as rapidly as they had arisen.

"Why, Elisabetta. Why? Why? How could you do this to me?" He slumped into a chair and began to weep. He was on his way back down. She nodded to Danilewicz. She moved to Frank and put her arm around him. She was not sure whether one minute or twenty passed, but soon Michael quietly came into the apartment.

"Come with me, Francesco," Michael said when he approached. "We'll go to the doctor. There is a very good one at Bellevue."

And so it began.

1932

What should she do now? Elizabeth needed a plan.

She took Joseph and Vincent on a walk north on First Avenue, vaguely heading in the direction of Tompkins Square

Park. She had solved the Frank problem for the moment, thanks to her brother-in-law Michael, but what now? It had been only two days, but she could already feel the terror descending. She couldn't seem to put her thoughts in any sort of coherent order. She would see flashes of Frank's face tinged with sadness, anger, and madness at the most unpredictable moments. All her family—Dominick, Teresa, Adrianna—kept telling her that she needed to put him behind her. She couldn't argue with them; she needed them, if for nothing else but to pay the rent.

She walked past the St. Stanislaus Polish Church. Past the drug store with its advertisements for Zemo Creme and Lifebuoy Soap and even Kruschen Salts, which claimed to help you lose weight. *Oh, these Americans and their foolishness*, she thought. She felt a despair so deep that it seemed to emanate from within her bones. All the Zemo Creme in the world was not going to help her.

She was alone with her boys in a strange land far from home, penned in by the never-ending buildings all around her. She so missed the air and the sun and the hills of Itri. And she knew—she just knew—that things were only going to get worse.

I must find some air in this city.

Elizabeth continued down Seventh Street past the mortuary and entered Tompkins Square Park. She sat on a bench and tried to watch as Joseph and Vincent climbed the new playground equipment. She noticed a wrinkled copy of the *Daily News* in the trash and picked it up to distract her. Perhaps somewhere in the paper would be a sign or a message to tell her what to do next. Some way to stop the shadows that were rising all around her. She scanned the headlines:

- COLORED MAN IS INVITED TO HOOVER FETE — "The last time a colored person was a White House guest was on 13 June 1929, when Mrs. Hoover entertained Mrs. Oscar De Priest, wife of the Illinois Representative, at a tea for women of the congressional set."
- SNIFF NOT ENUF IN BEER RAID COURT'S RULING — "Prohibition agents must have something besides an acute sense of smell upon which to base brewery raid, Federal Judge William Bondy decided yesterday."
- HITLER'S DREAM OF CABINET POST COMING TRUE — "The spokesman emphasized, however, that the Cabinet would retain its so-called super-party character, relying on President von Hindenburg for support."
- EMPHATICALLY NOT JUST ANOTHER "LOW PRICE CAR" — "Women everywhere will be interested to know that Miss Amelia Earhart, who christened the Essex Terraplane, is the first woman in the world to own one of these new type cars."
- DECREE CHANGES COMMUNION RULE — "The Catholic Congregation of Sacraments has issued a decree declaring that confirmation must come before first communion at an age of not less than seven."

Ten minutes extended to about an hour, until she finally gave up. She put her head in her hands, begging for the pain to stop. Even in this park—in this tiny square of green—she could not escape the deep depression that engulfed her. All around her were signs of doom. The elm trees—most of them stripped of their leaves by the strange Dutch disease sweeping the city—all spoke to her in quiet tones of desperation, harbingers of the deathly shadows she saw at every turn.

From the very corners of the park, shadows from the past closed in on her, slowly but inevitably surrounding her. The hundred dead from the draft riots in the park during the Civil War—mostly colored and killed by the Irish—approached her. Interspersed with them she saw dead Sardinians and many Itri boys killed during the Great War. From within these shadows Frank emerged. His eyes stared at her, pleading with her, accusing her of abandoning him. Accusing her of treachery. Accusing her of his death.

She dropped her head in a prayer for even a moment of peace from the sorrow that engulfed her.

1932

Elizabeth sat in the courtroom in a trance. She listened to the doctors make their report.

"Excitable. Disoriented. Bewildered. No insight. Diagnosis: Dementia Praecox."

When her turn came, she tried to calmly tell her story.

"Mrs. Mancini, are you the petitioner for this commitment?" She glanced at her brother Dominick, not completely sure of the exact language, and he nodded his head very slightly.

"Sì, I mean, yes, your honor."

"Can you talk very briefly about your life with Mr. Mancini?"

Although Frank was still at the crazy ward at Bellevue, she could feel his presence. She could feel his dark eyes, the eyes that could penetrate her soul. She knew that what she was about to say would change things in ways she could not possibly imagine. But she needed to do something to protect Joseph and Vincent. She started slowly.

"For the last four years Frank has acted somewhat peculiar. He often comes home from work and beats me. Recently he has beat me more often. One day I saw him talk to himself. He spits a lot. About two years ago," she paused. It took every strength she could muster just to get the next few words out. "He had a convulsion."

"Thank you, Mrs. Mancini. And Dr. Colbert, have you had conversations with Mr. Mancini about this? What is your assessment?"

"Yes, we have, your honor. A transcript of Mr. Mancini's comments is in the filing."

The judge looked down to read the comments.

> I just argue with the landlord Saturday. For three to four years he always get his rent. We had argument just for nothing. I hollered at him. I don't know why. I started to holler myself. I never was much nervous. Nothing—I can't tell nothing. They take off all my blood; that's the life I got. Too much dirty in the street, the house. The woman want to be stronger than me. What kind of work I have to do myself. I don't know if it's the woman upstairs. My wife needs to be watched, have I got to be watched

all the time? I can't tell what I know; for three years I get no strength, I am so weak.

"Anything else?" said the judge.

"No, nothing else, your honor."

"Thank you, doctor," and the gavel came down. "I think we've heard enough to recommend commitment to the Rockland Asylum."

Elizabeth signed the court order. And it was done.

EIGHT

By just about any standard, the Rockland Psychiatric Hospital was a scary place. The pictures in a two-part photo essay on Rockland called *Scouting an Abandoned Mental Asylum: A Visit to the Rockland Psychiatric Center* by Nick Carr certainly make the place seem creepy. But what really grabs my attention are the comments made about Carr's two posts.

There are more than *400* comments between the two posts, many of which tell horrifying tales of loss and abandonment and frustration. Frustration that *no one* will tell these many sad people the story of what their relatives experienced.

- I grew up about 10 minutes from here and had family in the next town over. I never saw it up close but heard a few "escaped inmate" tales when I was young. It was always referred to with an eerie or scary slant.
- I believe my mother was born there in 1941 and I am unclear if her birth mother was pregnant when she entered it, or if she became pregnant under their care.

- I was never able to find out information about my twin brothers that were buried on the grounds. There were several different cemeteries, and throughout the years many of them either remained unmarked or were destroyed. That combined with poor record-keeping made it impossible to tell where exactly the remains of my two brothers were.
- My mother was told that her mother was abandoned by her grandparents and had a great deal of anger toward her and no interest in pursuing the truth. I always wanted to know what happened to her. The stigma about mental health caused a huge vacuum and the need to fabricate stories in my family. I imagine we are not alone.
- This place was right out of Cuckoo's Nest. I did my nursing psych rotation here in the 80s. There was a metal door locked behind you everywhere you went. I was in a ward with men who had been institutionalized for many years. One guy was in his 40s at the time and had been there since he was a teenager. He started a fire, killed his family. Most of the men seemed to wander in circles.
- It was a difficult time in the treatment of psychiatric illnesses. Some of the treatments were very harsh and I cringe remembering being a part of them. Thorazine and Stelazine were just introduced. Many patients received insulin shock. I know there were many patients institutionalized

who didn't belong there, but then there were patients who were so sick that I couldn't imagine how they could live without some sort of protection that Rockland did offer.

On and on the comments go, cries for information about lost parents and siblings and grandparents and aunts and uncles. So, there was no fiery demise in the 1930s for my grandfather. But there was *this*.

I am not sure how he does it, but my partner in family history crime, my brother Joe, manages to get a 1932 medical record out of the Rockland State Hospital. Much in the record reinforces the information in the commitment papers.

Right before the commitment in August, the Bellevue people offered this summary:

> Well developed, poorly nourished, young white man, pupils react to light and accommodation. Hands cold. Heart and lungs negative. Knee jerks equally active. Spinal Wasserman negative; Blood Wasserman negative. [Note: These were syphilis tests.]
>
> Mentally, patient is tense, excitable, restless, irritable, and uncooperative at times. Attention is difficult to retain; he is fidgety. When questioned he is reticent and evasive. He expresses hypochondriacal

and persecutory ideas. He is partially disoriented and somewhat bewildered.

The record reports "a faint trace of albumen in the urine," which is an indicator of underlying kidney problems, and "marked cyanosis of both lower extremities." Peripheral cyanosis is a condition in which the extremities develop a distinctive bluish discoloration because they are not receiving enough oxygen-rich blood. It's not usually serious but can be an indicator of underlying heart/circulatory problems.

The report goes on to explain that in Frank's two months at Rockland, things had gotten worse. Quite simply, the doctors at Rockland had reached a conclusion about Frank that likely pre-determined his future:

> State of New York—Department of Mental Hygiene
> Rockland State Hospital
> 18 October 1932
> We have a psychosis in a young man of 34 with a fairly typical pre-psychotic schizoid personality who has shirked his responsibility in supporting his family during the past four years. In spite of several jail sentences for non-support of his family this did not seem to have any marked effect upon him. For no sooner was he taken out than he would slump back again to his old ways, remaining at home and refusing to work. As a result, a number of arguments ensued between the patient and his wife which finally wound up in a fight—the patient striking or beating her. As time went on, he

developed paranoid delusions that his wife was in league with the landlord, as well as the fact that she attempted to poison him.

He attempted to assert his authority in the home by insisting that he was boss, becoming excited and quarreling and which ended in beating her up. During the past year he has shown memory defects and has been forgetful. Prior to his admission to Bellevue 6 months ago he became sexually impotent and developed ideas of infidelity against his wife.

Since his admission he has shown very little improvement, maintaining his impulsiveness, hyperactivity, and elated mood. At times his conversation is rambling and somewhat disjointed. He expresses the idea that it is foolish for his wife to come see him, and it is better for her to be with the children. He feels that she has no business here.

He still expressed ideas of infidelity and paranoid trends directed against her. There is no evidence of hallucinations, either auditory or visual. His physical condition is good. He helps with the ward routine, although at times it is necessary to coax him to have orders carried out.

Diagnosis:	Dementia Praecox, Paranoid type
Condition:	Unimproved
Prognosis:	Guarded
Treatment:	Institutional care, occupational and social therapy

Dr. A.M. Stanley
Clinical Director

NINE

Belle parole non pascon i gatti.
Fine words don't feed cats.

FRANK AND ELIZABETH, 1932

Their tiny apartment felt like a tomb. Elizabeth's demons chased her, and she worried they were gaining ground. Her dread of the future would not leave.

What if she was wrong? What if sending Frank away was not her chance to escape, but her punishment for her faithlessness? Do we each create our future, or do we just fulfill it? How had Rita been able to survive the terror of her own Mancini? How did she get up each morning?

She needed to see Frank.

Elizabeth sat in the waiting room listening to the cacophony of voices all around her, a few in English, the rest in Italian or Polish or Russian or Yiddish. And others that she had never heard before. She was waiting her turn to see Frank.

It had taken a subway and then a train and then a bus to get to Rockland. All along the way, she felt that everyone was looking at her, looking through her. She felt that everyone knew her secret, knew what she had done; *She had committed her husband to an insane asylum.* And now she was not sure what to do. As she passed through the imposing iron gates engraved with capital *R*, she had an icy foreboding that chilled her.

As she waited for them to call her name, she prayed to Rita, aware more than ever of the irony of her prayers. This kind of situation had not exactly turned out well for Rita. Rita's husband—Paolo *Mancini*—had been killed and then she had been forced to give up her sons to save them from eternal damnation. And yet to whom other than Rita could she turn? Elizabeth prayed:

> Oh glorious St. Rita, obtain for me the grace to suffer with resignation the troubles of this life, and protect me in all my needs. Be kind to me, for the greater glory of God, and I promise to honor thee and to sing thy praises forever. St. Rita, you are the patron of the impossible. You were greatly burdened during your life and you know what we are going through now. I offer my prayers for relief, please hear and answer me.

Ten minutes in the waiting room stretched into thirty, which stretched into an hour. Still, all the accusing eyes fell upon her, and she felt a darkness descending upon her like a shroud. A darkness that she had to consciously shake off. She needed to stay here, in the present. And finally, her name was called.

She was led into a room colored in strange pastel shades. She wondered if this had something to do with calming the people who were there. If it did, it certainly was not working. There were tables across the middle of the room. Those visiting were placed on one side, and the patients, or inmates or prisoners, on the other.

All around her were small clusters of visitors and inmates. Periodically, a shriek would go up from one group or other, and the guards would descend to restore order. Order meant quiet muttered conversations, no touching, and an uneasy truce with the demons that resided in this place.

Frank came in and sat down across from her. At first, neither of them said anything. She looked closely at him, looking for signs of her Francesco. For a moment, she thought she saw something, but then he immediately retreated, and a darkness came into his eyes.

"What am I doing here? Why am I here? Why can't I leave?" His words came tumbling out in Italian. His eyes darted furtively back and forth, back and forth around the room. He could barely sit still in his chair. Elizabeth recognized the signs, the mania, and steeled herself.

"Frank. Don't you remember? The fights at our apartment? The big fight in August when Michael brought you to Bellevue?"

"What month is this? How long have I been here?"

"It's Octo—"

"It is your fault I am here," he interrupted in rapid Italian. "You just want to be the boss. You and that landlord, trying to poison me so that you two can go off and take my children. These people here. They never let me out of their sight. Are they reporting back to you? Are they your spies? Or perhaps they are spies for that damnable Pollack from next door? Always watching. Always watching. Always trying to poison my food. And here, too. But I smell everything! And I eat nothing with the smell of pineapples and pepper! Nothing!" On and on he went, hopping from one disjointed topic to another, gathering speed and intensity as he switched from topic to topic.

"*Porca puttana! Stronza! Baldracca! Zoccola!*" he screamed and then he lunged at her, swinging wildly.

And then it was over. The guards descended. The fight drained out of him as quickly as it had risen, and he was ushered out of the waiting room.

Just another visit to Rockland.

1934

With each day, her guilt compounded like a snowball gathering force and size as it rolls down a hill.

How could she have done this thing? How could she have sent her Francesco away? Where did her lifelong anticipation of sorrow come from? Why couldn't she shake it? How could she go on?

But worse than that, she also wondered how many sorrows she had brought upon *herself* and brought now upon her children. After all, she was the one who had signed those papers. They had all said it was for the best, but was it? God did not bring injustice to the virtuous, and He did not make mistakes. That meant there must be something about what she had done that displeased Him.

With each week, her own shadows were growing. How to get through the day? How to keep the creditors at bay? Even with the help from the city, how to pay all of the bills?

Rita, now would be a good time to answer my prayers.

Every Monday, Wednesday, and Friday afternoon, Captain Tim Healy gave Joseph something to look forward to. Joseph counted down the minutes until 5:45 and the *Ivory Stamp Club of the Air*. Joseph loved the way Captain Tim used stamps to tell incredible stories of lands far from their small apartment and far from the sadness that seemed to surround the three of them. Captain Tim especially liked stories about spies. Joseph thought he might become a spy someday, trusting no one and keeping all his secrets to himself.

One day, Captain Tim promised a big announcement.

"Vinnie. It's a big day today. Captain Tim will be making an announcement," Joseph told his brother. Vinnie was not nearly as excited about Captain Tim as Joseph was, but he went along and sat down next to his brother in front of the radio. Joseph jiggled the knobs and carefully tuned the radio to WEAF, number 660 on the dial. A booming voice came through the tiny speaker as if right on cue.

> Hello, boys and girls, this is your old friend, Captain Tim Healy. And welcome to this very special episode of the *Ivory Stamp Club of the Air*. Because today, we will finally become a true club. A club for all of you adventurers out there, a special club. So

pay close attention, because I'm going to give you all of the details and I don't want you to miss them.

Joseph leaned forward to catch every word. Vinnie did so as well, more as a show of support for his brother than as an expression of interest in whatever this stamp club was.

"Joseph, when will this radio show be over? It is almost time for dinner," interrupted Mama. There was an edge to her voice. *This was not the time for an interruption*, Joseph thought. Captain Tim was sending a special message to him! But it also was not the time to get Mama angry. "Yes, yes. Just a few minutes, Mama. It will be over at six." She sighed and returned to the stove.

"I would like all of you to get a pencil and paper while I tell you a little about Ivory Soap," said Captain Tim with some degree of urgency. "Vinnie, you keep listening," said Joseph. He ran off to get the pencil and paper.

> I want you to keep healthy and strong with Ivory Soap so you won't miss any of our programs. I always use Ivory Soap—and I recommend that you do—because Ivory is absolutely pure. It makes you skin feel smooth and refreshed; it rolls off the dirt in a jiffy. And then, too, Ivory floats! You don't have to dive underwater to find it. It is right ready by your hand. Keep healthy and strong with an Ivory bath every single day.

Joseph came breathlessly back into the room and skidded into place beside Vinnie. "What did I miss?"

Vinnie echoed back Captain Tim's final piece of advice: "Keep healthy and strong and take an Ivory bath every single day."

"What!?" Joseph lived for Captain Tim's advice and guidance, but this was crazy. "Every day?" he said to Vinnie. "Are you sure he didn't say every Saturday?" Captain Tim had started to speak again. "Never mind. We'll figure it out later. I'm sure he meant every Saturday. Nobody takes a bath every day."

> I am happy to announce the Ivory Stamp Club of the Air, a real club, and I want each of you to become a member of my special club. I know we are going to have a wonderful time in this club. Stamp collecting is one of the finest and most interesting of pastimes. Not only boys, but girls too, and grown-ups as well as youngsters, get a world of pleasure from it. Stamp collecting is the ideal hobby for young people of all ages!

I am pleased to tell you that I have reserved for each of you your very own stamp album. You will need to send me two wrappers from Ivory Soap and a nickel to get started. Now write down this address, it's an easy one to write down. Captain Tim read off the address in his big booming voice. "Captain Tim, Box 1801, Cincinnati, Ohio."

Joseph scribbled the address down on the paper.

So here is your assignment. Ask your family and friends if they have any Ivory Soap wrappers, and to start saving the wrappers whenever they open a bar of soap. Send two of the wrappers and a nickel to the special address I just gave you, and I'll immediately send you your very own membership badge, stamp album, and 50—yes fifty—stamps. Imagine the exciting and interesting stories that these postage stamps will tell—stories of intrigue and spies and adventure from all around the world. Just like the stories I tell you each time we're together.

Every day Joseph asked whether his package had arrived. "Mama what was in the mail today? Did Captain Tim send me my stamp album? He promised that if I sent him a nickel and two Ivory soap wrappers, he would send it." Mama was skeptical about the entire arrangement.

But then the day arrived. There was the package. Joseph opened it and inside was his own stamp album. It was something no one could ever take away. Something that was only his. It had a blue cover with the words the "Ivory Stamp Club with Captain Tim Healy" in big blue letters on the front, and a gigantic picture of Captain Tim himself in his military uniform.

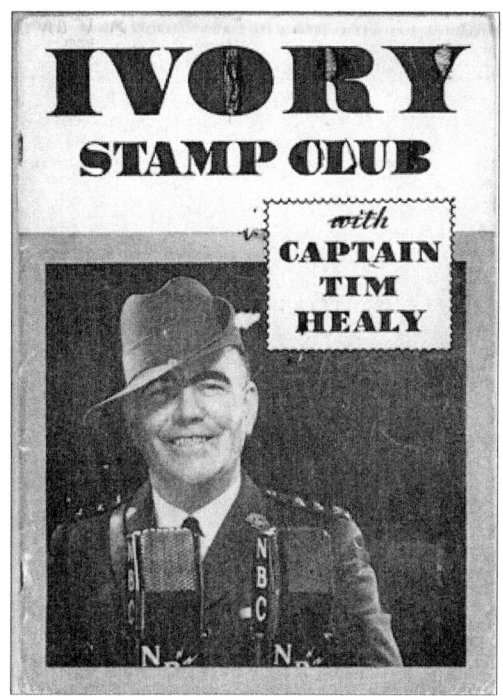

He opened the cover and there it was . . . a message from Captain Tim—a message just for him.

> As we turn the pages of the Ivory Stamp Album, you will find that we can go adventuring All Over the World—yes, and even backwards into history—by means of the interesting and exciting stories that postage stamps tell—the stories that lie behind the stamps!

Joseph looked at the clock on the wall and realized that it was 5:45. He had almost missed the show.

> Boys and girls, all of you future spies out there, all the members of the *Ivory Stamp Club of the Air*, I

want you to do me a favor. I want you to show your Ivory album to all your friends. Tell them how easy it is to join the Ivory Stamp Club. Show them the big list of stamps that you can get in exchange for Ivory soap wrappers and be sure to listen regularly to the Ivory Stamp Club program and my offers of many different stamps for your album.

If you are in school, take your Ivory album to class with you; and ask your teacher to help you to form a stamp club in your school or classroom. Teachers everywhere are becoming interested in stamp collecting, because it makes history, geography, and other subjects so interesting. A school stamp club is lots of fun and it also gives you an opportunity to trade stamps with other collectors. It's easy to start a club!

Joseph could not believe that Captain Tim had invited him to become part of the club. For a few moments, he imagined floating above their tiny apartment, participating in incredible adventures in other countries, acting as a spy on behalf of Captain Tim. Captain Tim often talked about the secrets that spies needed to keep, of things they could tell no one for fear of jeopardizing all the people they loved. Joseph thought, *I have been doing this all my life.*

"Today's adventure takes place in Northern Italy," Captain Tim said.

Northern Italy? thought Joseph. He couldn't believe it. The place where his family was from!

Captain Tim continued:

If you could, turn to page 35 and read along with me. I'd like to tell you a little bit about Italy before I talk about today's spy adventure. Italy is one of the great nations of the world. This is due in large measure to its warm sunny climate, which permits farming year-round, and to the thrifty and industrious character of its people. Italy is one of the foremost European countries in the production of wheat, which in the form of flour is used in the manufacture of macaroni, the national food of the Italians.

Captain Tim continued to speak, but Joseph drifted off, lost in his own thoughts.

Thrifty and industrious? thought Joseph. *Thrifty and industrious?* He only said the words to himself, because he knew that they were not true about his own father. He remembered all the whispers just a few years ago. *He will not work. He drinks too much. He beats his wife.*

And then that day when they came for Papa, and they took him to the hospital. After that no one would say anything. It was as if Papa had vanished into thin air. And every time he tried to ask about him, everyone—even Mama—would start talking about something else. At first, that was all they did; they just switched the subject. And then more whispers. *We will never mention him again. He is gone forever. Those boys are better off without him.*

Each time before the people from the city came to their apartment to check on them—apparently the ones who gave them money—Mama would gather Joseph and Vincent together. They would all quickly go through the four rooms of their apartment, straightening things out and making sure everything was clean. She would remind them how they were to behave and how they were to answer questions. "We must do the things these investigators expect and say the things they want to hear if we are to get Papa back."

He knew, even though he couldn't really understand it, that they were in trouble. Joseph could hear Mama crying in the night. There were nights when he seemed to be the only one available to take care of Vinnie. There were nights when he wished things could just go back to the way they were. But now Papa was gone. That's all there was to it. That was the beginning and the end.

He imagined all the fellow stamp collectors and fellow spies out there, ready to help him if he could only find them and contact them. Perhaps the club was the way.

They said that Papa had "disappeared," and would say nothing more. It was a while before Joseph understood what this meant. Uncle Michael—Aunt Jennie's husband—had also "disappeared." Well, that's what they had said at first. Aunt Jennie was the one who had told him what had really happened. "Your Uncle Michael has died, Joseph. Some will say that he has just disappeared. But you are old enough to know the truth, Joseph," his aunt told him. "Uncle Michael got sick, and then his heart could not get better, and he died. That is why everyone is so sad. That is why no one is willing to talk about what happened to him. But you are old enough to know."

And with those few words, Joseph knew what had happened. *Uncle Michael had disappeared. And Papa had disappeared as well.* Even someone who was not a spy for Captain Tim could figure out that puzzle. *Papa is dead*, he said to himself, quietly so that no one else could hear.

I must take care of things. I must take care of Vinnie. I must take care of Mama. I must make sure that Mama doesn't get sadder or else her heart will get sick like Uncle Michael, and she will also disappear. I must protect Vinnie from all of this; He is too young to understand.

Without even realizing it, the show was over. Joseph took his stamp album, and his membership pin, and his fifty new stamps and went to the corner and started matching the stamps to the pictures in the album. He was reassured by the order in the album, how every stamp had a place, and every stamp matched a picture. And stamp by stamp, he started to build his own world, a world in which people did not just disappear—a world in which Mama wasn't crying in the middle of the night—a world without so many secrets. *I'll be a good spy and keep all the secrets to keep my family safe.*

1937

Elizabeth prayed and prayed for deliverance. As the time stretched out between her visits to Frank at Rockland, each one worse than the time before, she realized her life likely would not return to the normal they had known in the years just after Joseph and Vincent were born. A husband in the crazy house, ranting at shadows and persecutors, consumed by his sense of injustice that his greatness had been denied by all whom he thought loved him was her normal.

All of this was her fault. *She* was the one who had signed Frank's commitment papers. She prayed that she could somehow undo everything and go back to how things were, no matter what that turned out to be. Certainly, things couldn't be worse than they were now. But her prayers went unanswered. Even the patron saint of lost causes seemed to have no time for Elizabeth. Surely, Rita, who had suffered with an intolerable husband of her own—and what are the odds, a husband also named *Mancini*! —would give her guidance. Surely, she would tell her what to do next, how to get out of bed in the morning and take care of her sons, and how to live. Every day she went to Mass. Every day she prayed. Every day she begged Rita to appear to her, to ease her pain, and to restore her peace. And as these prayers became more and more insistent, they took on a life of their own.

With both Joseph and Vincent at school, Elizabeth would sit for hours, staring at the same walls and at the pattern in the linoleum floor that had once given her such joy. All the items around the small kitchen seemed coated in a dust that only she could see, a dust of deep despair.

Frequently, her sister Teresa would stop by and check in on them. Most days, Elizabeth was able to hide her thoughts, hide the reality of her despair. Teresa's presence would prod her into completing the day-to-day tasks that she was neglecting. The routine of washing clothes, mopping the floor, doing the dishes, preparing lunches for Joseph and Vincent and then supper when they would come home from school—over and over and over—was too much for her.

Teresa knew immediately that this was an unusually dark day for Elizabeth. Teresa arrived shortly after Vincent and Joseph had returned to school after their lunch break. The kitchen was a wreck, with scraps of food scattered all over the place. Elizabeth had been washing the same two plates over and over, unable to imagine what on earth she should do next. The heat in the tiny apartment was unbearable because Elizabeth had neglected to open any of the windows that morning.

"Elizabeth, look me," Teresa commanded, more forcefully than she intended. Elizabeth continued washing her two plates. Teresa watched silently as Elizabeth carefully dried the plates, and then put the plates back into the sink, beginning the process all over again. Teresa gently took hold of Elizabeth's shoulders and turned her toward her. Elizabeth looked away, desperate to avoid her.

"Elisabetta," she said, using the name Elizabeth so missed, her given name that reminded her of a gentler time. Teresa let the command and judgement drop from her voice, and quietly pleaded, "You must gather yourself. Before the boys get home this evening."

Elizabeth stared blankly at her, hoping for instructions on how to do just that.

Teresa handed Elizabeth a quarter. She noticed it was one of the newer ones, the quarter with an image of George Washington instead of the standing woman holding the shield. She had peered closely at the image, waiting for a hint as to what might come next.

"I want you to go down the street to the cinema," Teresa said. "The matinee will just be starting. It will be cool in there. Do not think about any of this for a few hours."

Elizabeth nodded, still staring at the quarter. "In God We Trust" were in tiny letters under Washington's chin. Without even thinking, she looked up at Teresa and softly mouthed, "*Crediamo in Dio. Crediamo in Dio.*"

"Yes, yes, of course, Elizabeth. Now go. I will be here when you return. Between now and then you must pull yourself together." And with that she pushed Elizabeth out the door.

Elizabeth held the quarter tightly, muttering, "In God We Trust," and then in Italian, "*Crediamo in Dio,*" as she walked down the street toward the theater. All around her people were going about their business, going to and from—somewhere.

Her thoughts snowballed, round and around in an ever-increasing cycle of despair as she wandered toward the theater. *What has my life become? What would happen to Joseph and Vincent if something happened to me? I am all they have.* A snippet of an Italian lullaby came into her head:

> *Ninna nanna, ninna oh*
> *Questo bimbo a chi lo do?*

> Lullaby, lullaby, lullaby, ooh
> Who will I give this baby to?

Who? Who? Who? She must speak to Teresa about the boys. She must make plans. She must make plans. She must make plans. She must…

The elevated train above her roared by in a cacophony of sound that startled her out of her fog. *Ah yes,* she thought, looking down at George Washington on the coin in her hand. *The cinema.* She looked up at the marquee over the doors and almost laughed out loud as she snapped out of the endless conversations in her head and read the name of the movie, *Seventh Heaven,* starring Simone Simon and James Stewart.

Elizabeth settled into her seat in the enormous theater and breathed a deep sigh of relief. She was glad for the escape, even though it was only a temporary one. Every day the same. Worries about money. Worries about Joseph and Vincent. How would they survive with Frank locked up? How would they pay the rent? Was Frank gone forever? What would they do if he came back? Round and round, the same thoughts, the same worries, the same sense of a darkening cloud.

The newsreel was describing Japanese attacks in China at a Shanghai train station. The booming English voice of the narrator was a bit fast for her, and she struggled to follow. But the image at the center of the film seared into her heart. A tiny crying baby—was it a boy or a girl?—with tattered clothes and burned skin, sat amidst the rubble of a train station. Everywhere around this poor child was horror. She felt the tears roll down her cheeks as she said a prayer asking no matter what happened to her, that Joseph and Vincent be spared from such a fate.

Once the actual movie began, it was difficult to follow the English conversations. Elizabeth concentrated hard on the images on the screen to know exactly what was going on. As she concentrated on the film, she began to feel some of the tension leave, and the endless conversations that ran in a loop inside her head were replaced by the ones on the screen.

A man named Chico, played by a tall actor with kind, deep set eyes, prayed to God that he might be promoted from sewer worker to street cleaner, a prayer that perpetually went unanswered. Chico pleaded, "I have prayed so long and so loud that even if He was deaf, He must have heard me."

Kýrie, eléison (Lord have mercy), Elizabeth thought.

A kindly priest then gave Chico responsibility for a young woman named Diane, who was tortured by an evil sister running a bordello. When the police went to arrest Diane, Chico stepped in and said she was his wife and rescued her from jail. But she was still a desperate woman, and thought suicide was the only way to escape her fate. Chico asked Diane, "Why do you want to take your life?"

"I've had enough of it," she replied.

Christe, eléison (Lord have mercy).

Chico's friends were drafted to serve in the army in the Great War. Diane prayed that Chico would marry her for love, not pity. Elizabeth was amazed at how determined this Chico was to save Diane. He apparently would do *anything* to save her, including marrying her. He said, "Marry me, and then you'll be free. And you can be yourself."

"Myself, who would that be?" she asked.

Chico married Diane and then proclaimed, "Chico ... Diane ... Heaven," turning it into not so much a declaration as a prayer. Shortly after they were married, Chico was also drafted and sent to the front. Diane prayed for his safety and for a sign that he was indeed safe. They had agreed that each day, at eleven in the morning, they would both pray: "Chico ... Diane ... Heaven." In doing so, each day they sensed the other's presence and safety.

Kýrie, eléison (Lord have mercy).

Until one day, Diane failed to feel Chico's presence. She felt … nothing. But Diane still did not give up. She still believed that God would spare him.

She prayed Chico would return. And in fact, Chico was not dead. He had been blinded in a poison gas attack, but he was alive and returned to her.

Francesco...Elisabetta...Itri, Elizabeth chanted to no one in particular. Elizabeth felt her thoughts wander back to the warmth of Italy, to the time when she first fell in love with her Francesco. To the time when their lives had not yet gone so awry. But almost as quickly as these thoughts came to her, they were overwhelmed by the shadows of 1932. Shadows that would not disappear, shadows that she in fact had brought on herself. Shadows that she always had known were there. Her destiny.

Frank...Elizabeth...Commitment

In the darkness of the theater, Elizabeth prayed for the strength to survive. She prayed for a sign that she was not alone.

As the credits rolled and as the lights came on, she caught a glimpse out of the corner of her eye.

Rita.

TEN

A confession. Back when I found Elizabeth in the 1940 census, *she was also listed as an inmate at the Rockland Asylum.* And so, as I sit in the records room at the New York Supreme Court, I actually hold *two* accordion commitment folders in my hand, one for Frank and another for Elizabeth. I initially think there must be some sort of mistake. What are the odds? *Two* mysterious grandparents who *both* wind up in the Asylum?

When I requested the 1932 records for the commitment proceeding for Frank, I also asked about Elizabeth and discover there are records for *her* commitment proceeding as well ... record number 13229 from 1938.

After reviewing Frank's commitment papers, I pause to contemplate what on earth happened between 1932 and 1938 to send Elizabeth down the same path as her husband. I wonder who committed her. I wonder how my father survived it all.

I reach into the accordion folder, and strangely there is an envelope inside. Elizabeth's name is written on the left in very nice handwriting. In the upper-right corner of the envelope are these words:

"New York County Clerk's Office, Copy of Commitment, Sealed by Order of the Court, Section 74: Mental Hygiene Law."

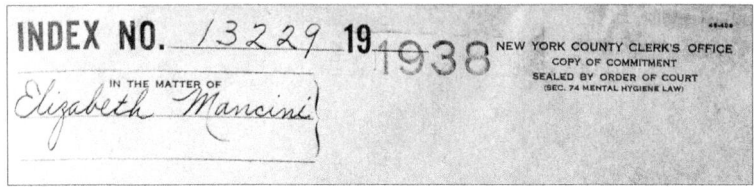

It is sealed.

I ponder sliding my fingernail under the envelope flap and ripping open this envelope, which has been sealed for over eighty years. The fact that I've spent the past twenty years working in records management and my respect for the law—and the possibility of cameras—pull me up short.

My merry chase for Elizabeth's commitment records seems to grind to a halt.

Fast-forward a year. A friend of mine tells me that in New York, *commitments for incompetency are sealed for 75 years.* It turns out I wasted a year and should have followed my instincts and just opened the envelope while I was in Room 103B. And so I begin the whole New York Supreme Court records retrieval process all over again.

I wait for what seems like weeks and weeks. Then one day I finally get my answer:

> We made multiple requests for Record number 13229/1938 from offsite records storage. I am sorry to report that the record cannot be found.

Checkmate.

Well, not quite checkmate.

Fast-forward *another* year, and on a Friday, shortly after the initial COVID restrictions ended, I get an email telling me that the long-lost commitment record I need for my grandmother—number 13229/38—has indeed been found and is available at the records room at the Supreme Court building in New York. The following Monday, I hop in the car and immediately head to New York, fearful that if I wait too long, they will lose the record again.

I repeat my path from two years before, winding my way through the security apparatus into the massive octagonal hall, likely still haunted by dementors, and down to the records room at 103B. I wait for some time at the counter for somebody to notice that I am there, even though there are many people behind the glass doing some sort of work. The staff is different from the first time I was there, and the sense of service I felt the first time I was there seems to have vanished.

Finally, with a bit of annoyance, someone hands me a brown accordion folder. It feels thinner than I imagined it would be. I find a table by myself, not sure whether social distancing rules are still in force, but even if they are not, I am not eager to sit at a table with anyone else. I settle down to look in the folder. As soon as I open it, I know the five-hour trip to New York has been a total waste of time.

Inside, there is no sealed envelope with a handwritten name Elizabeth Mancini in the upper left-hand corner that I had held in my hand two years ago. Instead, there is some sort of business incorporation document, totally unconnected with commitment or my grandmother or mental health. When the person who handed me the record passes by, I ask her if there is anything else that I can do, if there is any other course of action that she can suggest. She gives me a "Why don't you just go away" look.

Now admittedly I had been a bit of a pain in the ass in my persistence, although I believe I had exerted incredible self-discipline asking for this record only once every two months. I figure they might exhibit a little human compassion because this record—or more accurately, its absence—clearly is important to me, and I had gone to some lengths to try to find it.

"I *know* this record exists," I say. "I held it in my hand two years ago." I hold up my phone to show her a picture of the sealed envelope.

"You are not supposed to be taking pictures of these records," she snaps. "That's probably why you sat way over here in the corner." I have no idea what she is talking about. There are no signs prohibiting pictures of any records. In fact, there are ancient Xerox machines all over the place precisely for the purpose of duplicating records. Not to mention that two years ago, when I was in that exact same room, I sat at the main desk right across from the counter and made no secret of the fact that I was taking photos with my phone. No one cared.

I fear I am at a dead end in pursuing the commitment record, absent some sort of a miracle or change of staff. That means I am probably at a dead end in terms of understanding specifically what caused my grandmother to wind up in the Rockland Asylum in 1938.

I think back to the journey I took to find this one piece of information. I sent countless requests to records officials within the Office of Mental Health in New York State, who were pointedly unhelpful in providing health information to direct descendants. I sent copies of those emails to the state Assembly officials responsible for oversight of the records, all of whom ignored my requests. I sent many fruitless emails to hospitals and doctors' offices that might have somehow connected with my grandmother somewhere along her tragic path. I even contacted the doctors on my grandmother's death certificate to see if they had any records or any idea of what may have happened. I reached out to a handful of newfound relatives whose parents or grandparents were alive at the time my grandmother was alive, hoping that someone, somewhere might have some slight piece of information that would provide a clue. I even searched through comments on blog posts about the Rockland and Buffalo asylums and contacted commenters to see if any of them might have suggestions on where to turn.

After paying $48 for 90 minutes of parking, I find myself for the first time in this journey looking straight at a brick wall and wondering, "Does it really matter?"

It does, at least to me, if for nothing else than to satisfy my curiosity. But the other reason why it matters is that if I don't find out what happened no one will *ever* know, and my grandmother's story will be forever lost to history. And my grandmother's life will consist of just a birthdate and a wedding date and a few census records, without any knowledge of the life that must have been lived.

This unrecorded life must have mattered. It must have.

Records and Records Managers; I've learned that you never can tell what surprises they may yield.

Once I strike out on round two with the annoying New York State Supreme Court records people, I assume that I will *never* know the circumstances that surrounded Elizabeth's appearance in the 1940 census at the Rockland Asylum. And I think I have come to grips with having that gap in the story.

But I am wrong.

The New York Society for the Prevention of Cruelty to Children (https://nyspcc.org/) was a core source in solving the family history mystery (two newborns that wound up with the wrong parents) at the heart of Libby Copeland's *The Lost Family* (Copeland, Libby. *Lost Family: How DNA Testing Is Upending Who We Are*. Harry N. Abrams, 2021). It strikes me that if things truly unraveled for my grandmother and her two sons, perhaps there might be some record of this with the Society. Perhaps someone lodged a complaint or a concern, and someone from the Society stopped by to investigate. Was there some record that I had yet to find that would provide some hint as to how or why Elizabeth was committed in 1938?

Even though the Society's offices are not open to staff during COVID, Chelsea Frank from the Society manages to find an index card that indicates that during 1938, the Society had indeed been contacted about Elizabeth, Joseph, and Vincent, case number 537127. She tells me that the card indicates that there are documents of some sort tied to my grandmother, but that she won't be able to find out what they are until the offices reopen.

```
537127                   MANCINI         3/21/38
                         Frank
                       * Elizabeth
                         Joseph
                         Vincent
```

On a Friday afternoon—after I had literally been searching for four years for the answer about what had happened to my grandmother—Chelsea sends me an email telling me that the index card has led her to 11 documents dated March through May 1938.

These 11 documents at last tell the story of my grandmother's slip into insanity—or at least what passed for insanity in 1938.

> Case file 13527, NY Society for the Prevention of Cruelty of Children
> 21 March 1938. Miss Priscilla Bourbonnais from the Board of Child Welfare called us [the Society for the Prevention of Cruelty to Children] on the phone and stated that the Board has been assisting Mrs. Mancini since the commitment of her husband to the Rockland State Hospital in 1932. Since January 1st of this year, however, Mrs. Mancini has refused to accept any checks from the Board and there are now two checks of $55 each and another that will be issued in a few days waiting for her to receive them. The only reason Mrs. Mancini gives

for refusing the money is her belief that if she continues to refuse aid, her husband will be released and returned home.

Mrs. Mancini refuses to see workers from our office or to allow them to enter her home. The landlord has also been unable to enter the apartment and said that the rent has been paid to the landlord directly by a representative of the Board.

The Board asks that the Society assist them in having the mother sent to Bellevue Hospital for observation and possible commitment as insane, as it is believed from frequent observations that the mother is psychotic. Miss Bourbonnais also stated that the children are well fed, clean, and in no way neglected. She feels though, that the children are being affected by their mother's strange behavior.

ELEVEN

Ai mali estremi, estremi rimedi.
Desperate times call for drastic measures.

FRANK AND ELIZABETH, JANUARY 1938

After the visit in the movie theater, Rita's visits became more frequent, and Rita became more and more real to Elizabeth as the frequency of her daily visits increased. More real to her, in fact, than her own life, which slowly began to fade into the shadows. She *needed* to see Rita. She *needed* the solace of someone who had gone through what she had gone through. Who had two sons of her own. Who had married a crazy and violent *Mancini*. And gradually Elizabeth's thoughts tipped away from the real and more deeply into the fantasy.

"Elizabeth, I can see you are in pain."

"Oh, Rita, my life has become an intolerable thing. I have always known that sorrows would define my life. Sorrows that I could do nothing about.

"I have good news for you, my child. Your prayers have been answered, but first you must undo what you have done."

"How can this be?"

"There are forces seeking to destroy you. They lurk everywhere. You know they are there. I think you have always sensed the presence of these shadows."

"Yes, but what should I do?"

Rita prodded, "Where did all of this start, Elisabetta?"

"I don't know what you mean," Elizabeth replied tentatively, suddenly made uneasy by the use of the name from her youth.

"Of course you do. *You* signed the papers. *You* sent Frank away. And if *you* are not careful, *they* will take your children as well. Trust no one. Do not leave the apartment unless you absolutely must, because those seeking to lure you into traps are all around you. Do not sign *anything*. Trust in God, and no one else. Only by turning inward can you save yourself and your children."

Every day, Elizabeth had a similar conversation with Rita. At times she found herself speaking aloud, much to the concern of her family. At other times the conversation would be in her head, unknown to anyone but her.

She began to talk to her children about her visits with Rita. She was careful to do so only when nobody else was around.

"Do not worry, children. Help is coming. We will not be forsaken. Rita will be with us." Joseph was old enough to know that there was something strange about these conversations, and when his mother would start down this path, he would try to divert her to other things. He would talk about Vincent, about school, about the neighbors, about anything.

Over time, the conversations got longer and more rambling and more confusing and more frightening. Joseph would retreat further into his own world, focused on his stamps and coins and keeping Vincent safe. He worried about his father, whom no one ever discussed. How long ago had it been since he disappeared? So long ago…

FEBRUARY 1938

One day Elizabeth knew the time had come. *Her* time had come. She turned her precious keepsake box—the one she had been given by her parents all those years ago at confirmation—over and over trying to decide what to do. On each turn, she would pause to gently touch the two small hands hanging from the cross on the front of the box and pray for guidance and relief. This was not a new thing for Elizabeth; over the years she had worn the paint from the tiny hands.

She slid the panel open to reveal the hidden compartment in the middle of the box. The New Testament was long gone, but in its place was a collection of things, junk to anyone else but symbols of precious milestones to her: a menu from the Olympic; the tag that had been pinned to her when she first passed through Ellis Island; the letter that Frank had sent her all those years ago that had determined the course of her life; a small mass card from the baptism of Jack DeFabritus, her godchild; a pressed rose from her wedding bouquet; a few cards celebrating the birth of Joseph and Vincent; and the most recent addition, the ticket stub from *Seventh Heaven*.

"You know it's time," said Rita.

"But I can't." They were alone in the apartment; Joseph and Vincent were still at school.

"But you must," Rita quietly insisted. "Do you remember that it was only after I left my old life behind that I was allowed to become a nun at the Monastery of Mary Magdalene in Cascia?"

"Yes."

"It was only after I had demonstrated that I was worthy of this calling by putting to death my sinful nature through prayer and fasting and isolation. I had to leave my old life behind. Only then was I able to free my sons from the sins of their father and secure their salvation."

Elizabeth paced back and forth in the tiny kitchen, feverishly looking for a way to escape this penance. But when she turned to face Rita, she was gone. She was alone, like always, tightly holding her wooden box and pressing her fingers against the two tiny hands.

She opened all the windows in the apartment and dumped the few items from her box into a large pot on the stove. Elizabeth crumpled a few newspapers into the pot and lit another from the pilot light on the stove. While she waited for the paper to catch, she thought for a moment of leaving this crazy plan behind, walking out the door of their apartment and down the stairs to the street to clear her mind. She paused for a moment and then tossed the lit newspaper in the pot. Five minutes later, her few precious reminders of all that had been—a life she must leave behind—were gone.

"Let it be so," she said to no one in particular.

MARCH 1938

Elizabeth felt the forces gathering around her, simply because she had decided that only she could protect herself and her children. It had all started with a signature. A signature on that damn commitment paper that they had tricked her into signing. And now there seemed no way to undo it. But she knew that she needed to *start* by not making things any worse.

Every chance she had, she gave stern warnings to Joseph and Vincent. "Talk to no one. Trust no one. If anyone asks how you are, do not say anything. Say that you are fine."

But Joseph was old enough to know all was not fine. For reasons no one could understand, Mama refused the money from the Child Welfare people. Joseph had heard his cousins Mollie (Aunt Adrianna's daughter) and Rose (Aunt Teresa's daughter) talking. Mama wouldn't go to the offices to explain, and she wouldn't sign the checks. Mama simply refused to leave the apartment and grew more belligerent with each request. Joseph knew from listening to his cousins that the Child Welfare people were paying the rent directly, but beyond that, no money was coming into the family other than what he earned shining shoes. And the money was running out.

Although she knew the investigators were coming, and had prepared everything for their visit, when she heard the knock on the door on the 23rd, Elizabeth panicked. *I must hold firm*, she thought. *Now I must begin to undo what I have done and get Frank back. I must not sign anything; these people are not to be trusted. Someone has reported us, that is clear. Remember, they must think all is well and that everything is fine.*

Elizabeth took a deep breath and opened the door.

"Mrs. Mancini, my name is Priscilla Bourbonnais from the Board of Child Welfare, and this is Officer Cuoco from the Society for the Prevention of Cruelty to Children. May we come in?"

Elizabeth opened the door wide to let them come in.

"Why are you here?" she said. "As you can see, everything is fine." Indeed, as the officers looked around the apartment, everything seemed in order.

"Are your sons at home?" Miss Bourbonnais asked.

"Well, no. They are at school."

"May we sit and ask a few questions?"

"Yes," said Elizabeth, and she pulled out a few chairs from the kitchen table. *Here is where the interrogation begins*, thought Elizabeth. *Be very careful.*

"How are you feeling, Mrs. Mancini?"

"Fine, I have no complaint to make."

"Why are you refusing the money from the Board of Child Welfare to help support your children?"

"I am tired of all the investigators always coming by, looking for trouble, always questioning me."

"How have you been supporting yourself for the past three months?"

"I have saved some from my earlier allowances, and my son Joseph makes money shining shoes."

"Won't you please come by the office and sign the checks?"

"I will sign nothing. They all said I should sign the commitment papers for Frank, and it was a trick. It was all a trick. I am not going to be tricked into signing anything else, because it will mean that Frank will be forever locked up."

In the middle of all this, Joseph returned from school. Mama gave him a warning look, but that did not deter the investigators from turning to him.

"Joseph, do you know about the checks that we have for your family?"

"Yes, I do."

"Do you know why you mother refuses to take the checks?"

"I think she is afraid that if she signs the checks, something bad will happen to her or to us. Something bad like when my father was taken away after she signed to send him to that hospital. She won't even sign this check from the gas company for $5.55."

Joseph showed the check to the officers, and they noted that it was a check for an initial deposit to the gas company from five years ago and the interest that had accumulated.

"And even this she will not sign?"

"She is afraid. She thinks it's a trick. My cousins Mollie and Rose said they will go with us on Saturday to your offices to get the checks. I am sure my Mama will go if they take her."

As they were leaving, Miss Bourbonnais pulled Elizabeth aside, leaned over, and spoke softly. "Mrs. Mancini, you have nothing to fear from us. These checks have nothing to do with your husband and whether you sign them or not will have no bearing upon his release. Please go with your nieces on Saturday to get the checks. The money is needed for your children."

But no matter how much Rose or Mollie or Joseph or anyone else pleaded, Elizabeth was not going to be tricked again.

She needed to undo what she had done.

APRIL 1938

On Monday the 18th, the scene from the previous month was repeated, albeit with a different person from the Society. The apartment was clean and well-maintained. This time, Joseph was home, and appeared well-fed and cared for. The officer asked the same questions and got the same answers. Elizabeth was again asked why she refused to go to the Board to pick up the checks. All she could respond was, "I don't want trouble. If I go there, it will bring trouble. The signing was what caused the disappearance of my husband and brought all of these troubles upon us." Joseph assured the officer that his mother would call for the checks the following day, and despite the glare that Elizabeth gave Joseph, the officers left. Everything seemed a bit tense, but not dangerous.

During the time that it took the officer to reach the ground floor everything changed.

Loud screams came from the Mancini apartment. The screams were so loud that everyone in the building came out of their apartments to discover what was going on. The officer ran back up the stairs and burst into the apartment.

Joseph was standing at the window and screaming at his mother. "Mama, Mama, Mama you have to go and get the check. If you don't get the check they will come and get you. They will come and get you just like they took Papa. You must go get the check. You are being crazy. We have no money. We need more money than I can make shining shoes! If you don't get the check, I will jump out of this window and kill myself!"

Elizabeth screamed back at Joseph in Italian, lost in her own world. "I must undo what I did. I will never sign these documents of theirs, documents designed to trick us. Documents designed to land me in the same place as your father."

"But Mama," Joseph pleaded. "If you don't sign the documents, if you don't pick up the checks, that is exactly what *will* happen. They will come and they will take us away and they will take you away. You are all we have left!"

"Mrs. Mancini," said the officer. "How do you intend to buy food if you do not take the checks? You have no money!"

"That is none of your damn business," she screamed. "*Dio si prenderà cura di noi!* (God will take care of us!)."

"Mama, please!" yelled Joseph, stepping uncomfortably close to the open window.

Elizabeth picked up a hot iron and rushed toward Joseph, stopped only by the quick action of the officer, who grabbed Elizabeth and held her until her rage subsided. Joseph sat on the floor, eyes wide and terrified.

"Joseph, don't you think you should come with us? I worry whether you are safe."

He spoke quietly. "No, I will be fine. Mama was only talking. She will not hurt me. I will make sure she comes to the Board tomorrow to pick up the checks."

"Do you have anything to eat in the house?" he asked, a kind look in his eyes.

"I'll be fine," Joseph responded. "Hard boiled eggs and milk. She'll pick up the checks tomorrow."

But Elizabeth did not come in for the checks, so the officer called again at the apartment the next day. Elizabeth opened the door two inches and asked the officer what he wanted.

"Why didn't you go to the Board of Child Welfare yesterday like you promised? Don't you know where this all could lead?"

"That's none of your business," she hissed. "That is my affair."

"You need to go to the Children's Court tomorrow. They have issued a summons. You must go."

"I will not sign anything! That is where this all began! The only way Frank will be released is if I trust God and trust Rita and have nothing to do with you! *Dovrei ucciderti!* (I ought to kill you!)" She ripped the summons up and threw it back at him through the crack in the door and slammed the door.

MAY 1938

On Tuesday the 10th, Joseph and Vincent were summoned to the Principal's office at P.S. 105. They were aware that Mama had not left the apartment for the past two weeks, and spent her days by herself, speaking quietly to no one in particular. They were unaware that a string of summons had demanded the appearance of their mother in Children's Court, and unaware that Mama had ignored all of them. The 11th Precinct Police were asked to notify Mrs. Mancini that she needed to appear in Children's Court at once, and that her children had been taken into custody.

Elizabeth heard the banging at the door and saw yet another summons as it slid under the door. The shadows all around her overwhelmed her. She screamed, "I won't sign anything! I can't sign anything. *Sono da biasimare per tutto! Sono da biasimare per tutto!* (I am to blame for everything!)" And she collapsed in the corner, lost in a mumbled dialogue with Rita.

When Elizabeth failed to appear in Children's Court, a hearing was held. Officials from the Board testified that the children were neglected. Joseph and Vincent were temporarily remanded to the Society, and the case was referred to the Probation Department for investigation.

Elizabeth did not know how long she had been lying in the corner, lost in her private conversations with Rita.

When she awoke, she looked frantically around the apartment for Joseph and Vincent. She could tell by the light in the apartment that it was early morning.

Elizabeth dimly recalled the banging on the door from the previous afternoon and saw the summons lying on the floor. She saw "11th Precinct" on the top of the form and ran out the door to the Police Station.

"*Dove sono loro? Dove sono loro?* (Where are they?)" she screamed at the desk sergeant. "*Dove sono loro?*"

The desk sergeant left to find out what this crazy woman was screaming about, and as the time passed, she got more and more agitated. After 30 minutes, he finally got an answer from the Society.

"There was a hearing at the Children's Court yesterday, Mrs. Mancini. We attempted to inform you of the hearing, but no one answered the door at your apartment or responded to the summons."

She interrupted, "But what is this? I have been saying and saying that you people were out to get me. I have been saying that all the nonsense about signing these checks was designed to keep Frank in the crazy house. What does this mean? What does this mean? I do not understand! Rita warned me that I needed to stay away from you people. She promised that God would take care of me. Where are my children! Where are my children! What have you done with them?"

The officer spoke very slowly, making sure that Elizabeth understood what he was saying. "When you refused to show up at the Children's Court, they were placed by the Court in the custody of the Society."

Elizabeth stared at him; eyes glassy with fear. The hysteria overwhelmed her and she passed out and fell to the floor.

"Get a squad car," the desk sergeant barked to one of the other officers. "This one is crazy. Take her to Bellevue."

Six days later, Elizabeth was sent from Bellevue to the Central Islip Asylum, and effective May 25, Joseph and Vincent were placed in the temporary custody of their Cousin Rose.

It was Joseph's 13th birthday.

JULY 1938, CENTRAL ISLIP ASYLUM

It had taken Rose, Joseph, and Vincent two hours to get to Central Islip, even though a train ran directly to the Asylum. Elizabeth had asked to see Joseph and Vincent; she knew what she had to do, and she knew what she had to say. She had even asked permission to give her sons a gift.

They were still so young—Joseph was only thirteen and Vincent was ten. She looked into their huge brown eyes, fearful of the sacrifice that Rita demanded of her, fearful that if she was to save these children, she must follow Rita's example and sacrifice herself. In her eyes, they were still small children, vulnerable and dependent upon her.

Elizabeth peered into the kind eyes of her boys, knowing that the time had come. She slowly stood and gathered them close to her. "Come here. I have a story to tell you and a gift to give you." Rose looked at her curiously. But Elizabeth seemed so calm compared to the hysteria at the police station that she decided to remain silent.

"Back home, there once were two boys, not all that much older than you. And believe it or not, Joseph, one was named Giuseppe, which is what they call people with your name back home. He was a very smart boy, very much like you, and he had a little brother named Vincenzo, whom he loved.

"During the Great War, they were very afraid. They were afraid about talk of fighting and war, and about their father being off in the Italian army. They were afraid about how hard their mother was working to make sure they had enough food. They were so worried and so afraid that their mother knew she had to do something. So, she gave them a magic box.

"The box works like this. If there is something or someone you are afraid of, just draw a picture of it and then put it in the box. St. Rita is my saint, the saint to protect us from all scary things. The saint to pray to when you are afraid. She is very brave. And because she is so brave, you don't need to worry about what you put in the box."

"Thank you, Mama," they both said, uncertain about what might come next. Joseph and Vincent looked at each other, uncertain about Mama's tone, feeling like she was speaking to them as she would speak to a small child.

"You must not worry. Your father is not coming back to steal you. He will not hurt you. He will not hurt me. But I must ask you to help me."

"How, Mama? What do you need?"

Elizabeth handed Joseph the box that had meant so much to her, now empty of all her treasures. "Joseph, I must ask you to be in charge of the box."

Elizabeth prayed silently to Rita and the Madonna that what she feared was not true. She prayed that what she had always known would happen—what was predestined to happen—would not actually happen. She prayed that whatever Joseph placed into the box could not escape. That Rita would indeed be strong enough to keep Elizabeth's demons in the box and away from Joseph and Vincent.

Elizabeth handed Joseph a picture from her wedding day. She could barely remember the day, a fateful day that had led to this dreadful moment. "I want you to put the picture of your papa and me in the box. Keep us in there. It will keep us safe. But more importantly, it will keep you and Vincent safe. Do not let us out."

"Yes, Mama."

"We shall not speak of this again. It will be our secret."

And with that, after they left, Elizabeth entered a conversation with Rita from which she could not escape. It was an all-consuming conversation, at once comforting and terrifying. It was a conversation that she could not end.

1940, ROCKLAND ASYLUM

Elizabeth was uncertain how or why she was in this large room filled with so many beds. On each bed someone was talking, laughing, or sobbing uncontrollably, or occasionally screaming out obscenities. The ward nurses would come through periodically, alternating between words of encouragement and threats, anything to get everyone to shut up. Endless nights slipped into endless days.

Each day, Elizabeth would be ushered into a common area with the others. Patients were scattered all around the room. Some were sitting in a small ball in some corner or nook, others were flailing about, still others were staring out the windows through the grates at . . . something. They were all women, each with their own set of terrors that would be unleashed at the most unexpected times with a scream or a fit of uncontrolled weeping.

The voices. Oh, the voices. Mrs. O'Brien constantly circled the room in endless loops, asking everyone she saw whether anyone knew where her husband was. Mrs. Johnston was always agitated and ready for a fight. "That's my place! That's my seat! Who stole my cigarettes? This bitch is after my husband! My food! It's gone! I'm starving." Miss Goldschmidt was always looking for the doctors. When one would come through the ward she would move in quickly and accuse whoever happened to be in her path of touching her while she had been asleep. Myrtle moved about the ward continuously spelling her name: "M. Y. R. T. L. E." A tall, older woman recited the same story, over and over. Her husband accused her of having an affair. He beat her. She threatened to leave him, and he put her here. And that was that. She was not sure how many years ago. And then she would start the tale over.

Sometimes Elizabeth would hear voices coming to her from out of nowhere, unconnected to anyone. Accusing voices. Mocking voices. She would turn to confront them, ready to strike, only to flail at empty air. And then there were the tiny voices, vaguely familiar, poking and prodding at her consciousness, pleading and insistent. Always expecting her to do . . . something.

Elizabeth sometimes asked herself, *What am I doing here with all these misunderstood, misbehaved, and hopelessly confused souls, all living together in these crowded wards?* Then she would begin mumbling prayers that no one could understand.

Fortunately, Rita had followed her there. The visits from Rita were the only meaningful moments of her day. Only Rita remained faithful to her.

And then she, too, vanished.

TWELVE

With both of their parents listed as inmates in the 1940 census, where were my dad and my Uncle Vinnie?

They were fifteen and twelve when they showed up living at 55 St. Mark's Place in Manhattan. The building is still in the East Village between 1st and 2nd Avenue between 7th and 9th Streets on what is essentially 8th Street on the south side. They ended up living with my grandmother's sister Teresa and her husband, Frank Ruggieri, and their four kids. Elizabeth's other sister, Adrianna, her husband, Leonard Mancini (no relation), and their four kids were living in the same building. The list of missing relatives was beginning to resemble a village.

I was running out of Ancestry.com rocks under which to look. (Or in Ancestry terms, I was running out of family tree "leaves" to check out.) Then it occurs to me that I might find some information in my father's World War II enlistment papers for the Navy that might shed light on the story of my grandparents.

I request my father's military records for two reasons.

First, I really know virtually nothing about him from 1940 until he met my mom (1952) and married her (1953). I know he served in the Navy roughly from 1944 to 1946. Other than the quick glimpse of him in the 1940 census and living with his Aunt Teresa and Uncle Frank, I know nothing and really wanted to know more.

Second, I wonder whether the enlistment papers will reveal something about questions that had bothered me since this quest began, questions that sounded like something out of the Watergate files: What did my dad know? Was there any point at which he knew his parents were alive but institutionalized?

My brother and I always assumed that perhaps my dad was told by relatives as a child back in the early 1930s—maybe around the time they must have been institutionalized—that his parents were dead. The main reason for this assumption was that it stretched the boundaries of our imagination to think that he might have known as an adult that his parents were alive, and that he chose to walk away. Or maybe more accurately that he felt forced—out of self-protection—to *run* away. And if that was the case, what on earth must he have experienced as a young child to force him into this sort of self-protection?

Just when I think too much time has passed, and that I will need to start over, a package arrives, return address "National Military Personnel Records Center." I sense as I open the half-inch-thick envelope that I will learn something, whether I want to or not. There are many sheets—and many duplicates—roughly in reverse chronological order.

The Notice of Separation from the U.S. Naval Service notes that he enlisted on 4 April 1944 and was honorably discharged as a Yeoman 2nd Class on 23 May 1946. He completed a two-week Armed Guard School course in Norfolk.

His total payment upon discharge was $50.91. Even though I understand fifty bucks back then isn't fifty bucks today, it still seems like a small sum. Both the Foreign and Sea Service boxes are checked—aboard the USS *Simpson*. That is a piece of the story we had known for a long time. The *Simpson* was a four-stack destroyer left over from World War I, and largely served submarine duty on the eastern coast of the US and down into Central America.

He earned a Victory Medal and received the American Theater Medal. The family doesn't know what happened to them.

At the bottom of the form is my father's signature. He always signed his full name—Joseph John Mancini—and it gives me goosebumps to see his signature at twenty-one. It looks *exactly* like it did all his life. On a bunch of insurance forms, he lists his beneficiaries as his brother Vincent and Aunt Elizabeth DeFabritus (Dominick's wife).

There is a note saying he failed a night vision test with something called a radium plaque adaptometer with a score of 9 out of 20. That disqualified him from night lookout duties. He had always told us he was partially color blind, but I don't think we really believed him.

And after many, many copies of the vision test and much documentation of my dad's progression from Seaman to Seaman Second class to Yeoman Second Class, I come to the enlistment papers. A few facts pop up.

- He had never been (1) arrested or in the custody of the police; (2) in reform school, jail, or penitentiary, or convicted of any crime; or (3) on probation.
- He was five foot eleven inches and 168 pounds.
- His legal guardian was Elizabeth DeFabritus.

- He had worked for over five years as a part-time clerk, two years as a part-time delivery boy, and one year as a part-time newsboy.
- He had a high school diploma from Central Commercial High School, which opened in 1925, closed in 1975, and was located at 214 East 42nd Street.
- He could type thirty words per minute.
- Under leisure time activities, he listed collecting stamps and coins, beginning when he was nine.

Just when I think the entire exercise was a bit of fun but not terribly informing, there it is.

- Nearest living relative: Elizabeth Mancini, MOTHER.

Wait! What!? My father knew his mother was alive when he was eighteen?

That demolishes the idea that he didn't know she was alive. He did.

There is no mention of Frank, which is curious. I wonder what they told him about his father. And I wonder what dreadful experience could have led him to rope off and so compartmentalize his life that he never mentioned a *mother*.

There was another line, an address for Elizabeth:

- Buffalo State Hospital, Buffalo, New York.

BUFFALO?
What?

Episode 373 of the 99% Invisible podcast (*The Kirkbride Plan*) starts with a story about the Buffalo State Hospital:

> Maybe you have a story like this. How once upon a time, on the outskirts of the town where you grew up, or where you went to school, on the edge of the woods, there was a scary old asylum. But the one detail that almost never varies, the thing that seems to make an asylum story an asylum story, is that the asylum is nearly always… abandoned.

The first thing I notice coming up the drive to the Henry Hotel Resort Conference Center in Buffalo are two tall Romanesque red brick towers, each capped with green copper roofing. This impressive building—part of a larger campus—was designed by H. H. Richardson, an American architect known for his work in the Richardsonian Romanesque style. It was constructed in 1870.

Richardson, Louis Sullivan, and Frank Lloyd Wright are considered the Holy Trinity of American architecture. They are pretty heady stuff in architectural circles. And as if this wasn't enough to make the place preservation-worthy, the grounds were designed by the famed landscape team of Frederick Law Olmsted (the guy who created New York City's Central Park) and Calvert Vaux.

The building was abandoned and in decline until 2006, when the Richardson Center Corporation was formed with a mandate to save the buildings Richardson designed and to bring the campus back to life. After a period of political wrangling and stabilizing the buildings, the Hotel Henry—featuring the central building with the two Richardson towers and the two flanking buildings—opened in 2016.

That's where I stay on my trip to Buffalo to give a speech.

On my way to my room, I notice a beautiful mosaic floor—original to the building, my guide tells me—in a curious curved connector that leads to a wide hallway, adorned with a variety of original art. Room 215 is big and spacious and replete with precious design details that I'm sure have made it a favorite of the *Architectural Design* set. It is very fancy.

Of course, the *second* life of the property was not what drew me there, as fascinating as that was. It was the *original* life of the property as the Buffalo State Asylum for the Insane that attracted me.

If you look beyond the restored center Richardson towers and the two connecting buildings, there are four additional buildings on each side. The whole facility was built in the Kirkbride design, named after mental health innovator Thomas Story Kirkbride, and was considered a bit of a revolution at the time.

The concept was that environment—natural light and air circulation—were crucial to the treatment of mental illness. The idea was to have numerous wings that sprawled outward from the center. The men were located on one wing, and the women on the other. The reason for the wide hallways was to encourage patients to congregate outside of their rooms as part of their recovery.

Kirkbride facilities like the Buffalo Asylum were self-contained communities, providing a lot of their own funding and operating like small businesses, with vegetable gardens, greenhouses, dairies, livestock, and bakeries. Kirkbride believed that keeping patients occupied was key to their recovery. Patients therefore aided in farm work and other tasks regarding the daily operation of the asylum. Doing work was part of moral treatment, but so was amusement. Kirkbride facilities had ballrooms, bowling alleys, and baseball diamonds. One Kirkbride even had a pre-electricity roller-coaster.

Once you get past the two pavilions immediately connected to the central administrative tower, the condition of the remaining buildings declines precipitously. The buildings are still mostly in the condition they were in when abandoned, albeit with some structural reinforcement to keep them stable. It would be a crazy place to spend Halloween. Some believe the ghosts of patients still roam the hallways.

I don't know exactly how Elizabeth wound up at the Buffalo Asylum, but I guess it was because of overcrowding at the Rockland facility. I also don't know how long she was here, but I assume it was for a significant portion of her life.

Elizabeth arrived in the Buffalo State Hospital—the future home of the Henry Hotel Resort Conference Center—sometime between 1940 (when the census recorded her being at the Rockland Asylum) and 1944.

Looking at the annual reports for the hospital, I'm guessing she arrived in 1943. The number of transfers from other institutions averaged 23 per year for most of the early 1940s but spiked to 142 in 1943, which leads me to guess that Elizabeth may have been transferred in 1943.

Part of the reason for this spike was that the mental health system in New York did a good deal of shuffling during World War II. The forward-looking aspirations of the Kirkbride Plan died in a tidal wave of underfunding and overcrowding. According to the Asylum's 1944 annual report, "For the fifth consecutive year, the medical work of the hospital has been handicapped by the universal manpower shortage and the increased demands for psychiatric service caused by the World War."

The capacity of the hospital in 1944, as certified by the Department of Mental Hygiene, was 809 men and 1,133 women, for a total of 1,942. There were 1,052 men and 1,510 women at Buffalo when Elizabeth arrived, an overcrowding of 243 men (30% over certification) and 377 women (33% over). It was understaffed as well as overcrowded.

Like many hospitals for the mentally ill at the time, the Buffalo Asylum depended upon the vicissitudes of politics and the willingness of politicians to fund care. Even its first years revealed the tension. When the cornerstone was laid for the Buffalo State Asylum in 1872, Governor Hoffman touted the asylum as a "monument to State charity." Three years later Governor Tilden was elected and had this perspective on funding: "Why are we building palaces for lunatics?"

So why were these people institutionalized? Here's the list of reasons from the 1944 annual report.

	Male	Female	Total
General paresis	132	71	203
Alcoholic	40	14	54
Cerebral arteriosclerosis	81	79	160
Convulsive disorders	12	28	40
Senile	44	101	145
Involutional	28	87	115

Manic-depressive	18	79	97
Dementia praecox	617	926	1543
Mental deficiency	32	44	76
Everything else	48	81	129
Total	1052	1510	2562

Dementia praecox (in modern terms, schizophrenia) was the diagnosis that my grandfather had received, and I am guessing was the diagnosis that landed my grandmother at Buffalo. Poring a bit more over the annual report, I am drawn to a section on electroshock therapy, which was one of the primary treatments used to treat dementia praecox. Jack Nicholson in *One Flew Over the Cuckoo's Nest* comes to mind.

The report indicates that a typical treatment consisted not of one shock, but a series of 20 shocks. It also summarizes electroshock activities in 1944: "Treatments were completed on 345 persons: 127 men and 218 women. 113 men had one series, 11 had two series, and three had three series. 194 women had one series, 22 had two series, one had three series, and one had four series."

The numbers were up over the previous year because insulin shock therapy was discontinued in 1944 "due to staff shortages." Insulin shock therapy was a treatment in which doctors repeatedly injected patients with large doses of insulin to produce daily comas over several weeks. When they didn't have enough staff to do that, they increased electroshock therapy to fill the gaps.

An attendant from the 1960s offered this description:

They were still doing electric shock when I first went there. They were doing raw shock, and we held the clients down, they didn't give them any sort of sedative. The attendants were assigned to hold the patient down. Lobotomies were not going on at that point, that ended I think in the 1950s, although we did have patients who had had lobotomies. *(Farley, Buffalo State Hospital: a History of the Institution in Light and Shadow. Museum of DisABILITY History, 2015.)*

After reading many commentaries on places like Buffalo, I realize they all weren't horror movies. There were many people working on behalf of the patients. They tried as best as they could to deal with high patient-to-doctor ratios that were never intended. They tried to create a safe and self-contained community, providing places to work and live for people who just couldn't manage on the outside.

Many people in the first half of the last century were simply warehoused in asylums because they were poor or were recent immigrants. The numbers who were caught in a system they didn't understand or who were misdiagnosed (or all the above) is astonishing. Before we get too self-righteous and judge earlier standards of care too harshly, we need to consider how future societies will judge our decision in the 1980s to take a radically different course—to simply deinstitutionalize the mentally ill and throw so many of them out on the streets.

Among the thousands lost in mental institutions because of circumstances they didn't understand were Elizabeth and Frank.

On 25 October 2019, I finally make it to my first World Series game.

It took a while. It is only 24,493 days after my father made his only World Series appearance. As Terrence Mann said in *Field of Dreams*, "America has rolled by like an army of steamrollers. It's been erased like a blackboard, rebuilt, and erased again. But baseball has marked the time." Yes, 24,493 days is a lot of time marking.

The program for my dad's only World Series game—game three of the 1952 World Series between the Yankees and Dodgers at Yankee Stadium—has long had a framed place of honor in our home. Before I head to my first World Series game, I take the frame down off the wall, undo the clips on the glass frame, and leaf through the pages, looking for some sort of bizarre connection across the decades.

It is strange to hold a physical connection to my father. I immediately notice the size of the scorecard—it was only fifty pages and cost just fifty cents. Yes, time marches on.

I look online to find out how much the tickets were for the 1952 World Series, hoping that he had good seats. Seats in the lower deck for game three in 1952 were $6. For the Nationals 2019 appearance in the World Series, lower box seats are listed for $350 each, and going for $2,500 in the secondary market.

That might seem like a lot, but it has been 31,431 days since the last World Series game in Washington, DC. On 5 October 1933, the Washington Senators hosted the New York Giants in game three of the World Series. The Senators won the game, 4-0, behind a five-hit shutout from Earl Whitehill. Ultimately, the Giants won the World Series in five games.

Leafing through the program, I am struck that almost every advertisement is for either alcohol, cigars, or cigarettes. I am particularly drawn to the cigarette ads: "L.S.M.F.T. - Lucky Strike Means Fine Tobacco," "Where I come from, more and more folks say—For a TREAT instead of a TREATMENT smoke Old Golds," and "Nose, Throat, and Accessory Organs not Adversely Affected by Smoking Chesterfields."

The short player biographies seem amazingly familiar to me, even though all the players retired long before I was of an age to pay attention. I start scrolling through the pictures of all the Dodgers and Yankees listed in the program, all contemporaries of my father. The pictures strike a dissonant chord, a note that takes me a few minutes to interpret. Then it dawns on me. Five years *after* Jackie Robinson broke the color line only four Dodgers—and not a single Yankee—were black. It took another two and a half years—14 April 1955, 923 days hence—for the Yankees to sign a black man, Elston Howard. Yet another reason to dislike the Yankees.

The fifty-five players from those two teams, like the players in the cornfield in *Field of Dreams*—and for that matter, my father—are indeed *from another time*. Despite how curiously alive the names seem, only two—pitcher Carl Erskine and infielder Bob Morgan—are in fact still alive.

My father's scorekeeping comes alive in my hands. I know all the names in the lineup for a game that occurred 24,493 days ago, even though I don't know the names of the people who live next door.

Strangely, for both the Dodgers and Yankees, my dad started the lineups up one line higher than he should have, which means I have to jump one line down from each player's name to find out what they actually did in the game. My father used a very clean and straightforward scoring system. He recorded just the bare minimum of information for each at bat. A *W* for a walk. One, two, three, and four lines for a single, double, triple, and homerun. An *E* for an error and an *FC* for a fielder's choice. Fly ball to LF, just a *7*. Groundout to short, just a simple *6-3*.

The Yankees scored first in the bottom of the second inning. Hank Bauer walked and Billy Martin was intentionally walked on four pitches to get to the pitcher. Eddie Lopat promptly hit a single to score Bauer for a 1-0 Yankees lead. The

Dodgers tied it in the top of the third inning. Carol Furillo hit a double followed by a single by Pee Wee Reese, with Furillo winding up on third base. Then Jackie Robinson hit a sacrifice fly ball to drive Furillo home.

Billy Cox singled for the Dodgers in the top fifth. He advanced to second base on a sacrifice bunt by Preacher Roe and then scored on a single by Pee Wee Reese. Dodgers were up 2-1. They made it 3-1 in the seventh on singles by Jackie Robinson and Roy Campanella and a sacrifice fly by Andy Pafko. Yogi Berra homered in the eighth to make it 3-2, making him 3 for 4 on the day (single, double, homer).

My father weirdly communicates this directly to me through the miracle of baseball scoring. I can see the plays unfold before my eyes just through his simple pencil notations from more than half a century ago. The Dodgers scored two in the top of the ninth to go ahead 5-2. (Reese and Robinson singled. There were a pair of stolen bases and then a Yogi Berra passed ball allowed two runs.) Johnny Sain pinch hit for Lopat in the bottom of the ninth and homered, accounting for the third Yankee run in their eventual 5-3 loss.

How do these oddly familiar names pass directly through the years from my father to me? Just reading the scorecard allows me to imagine that I saw these long-dead Dodgers and Yankees play. I realize this wasn't just the result of old film clips played during the World Series and rain delays and the Ken Burns baseball special. I feel like I am reliving the game because my father talked about these players when I was growing up, talked about them as if they were *family*, talked about them as if he knew them, talked about them in the same way I talk to my family about players on the 2019 Washington Nationals like Ryan Zimmerman and Stephen Strasburg and Juan Soto.

And yet beyond the simple fact of his parents' names, his brother Vinnie, and a mysterious Aunt Jennie, in real life he never made any mention of his *real* family.

THIRTEEN

Vivere con seggezza.
Live with wisdom.

FRANK AND ELIZABETH, 1943

With the war, Rockland had gotten more and more crowded, and the pressure to move patients somewhere—anywhere—increased by the day. On her good days, Elizabeth would walk through the wards, looking looking ... looking ... for something. But she could not clear the haze in her mind. All she had was the sense that she should be looking for *something*. Or *someone*.

One morning, the nurse on the ward told Elizabeth, "We're going to go on a bit of a trip. Why don't you pack your things?" Elizabeth gathered her few personal items. She gazed at a picture of two small boys, struggling to understand exactly who they were and why she had this picture in the first place. She decided to leave it behind.

And that was that.

They put her on a bus and sent her to Buffalo, which was also crowded. There were so many people and so little privacy.

There were beds in the halls, multiple beds in the rooms, beds everywhere. And everywhere Elizabeth looked, there were sad eyes, eyes that seemed to bore through her, accusing her. She certainly felt damned. She certainly felt cursed. Her life had gone terribly wrong someplace—as she always knew it would. Whatever she had done, she needed to repent.

To escape the staring eyes, Elizabeth would sometimes walk outside and look upon the red brick walls and the two massive columns of the main building. The green copper-topped towers made it look like a castle. The towers seemed poised to reach down and grab her. They looked familiar, like something from somewhere else. Things that didn't quite belong in this place called Buffalo. This Buffalo where apparently there were no castles except this one.

She would walk around the circular path in front of the main entrance again and again. They said if she got better, she would move from building to building and then eventually out the front door. The three arched doorways at the front of the building confused her. *If my time should come, which one would I choose?* she wondered. She vowed to someday walk out the front door. And by then she would know which one to choose. Then she would find what or who she was looking for. If she could just get out.

Over and over, she wondered which door would be the right door as she went around and around the circular path, debating the relative merits of each door aloud. Occasionally she would pass people from the outside who would look at her with both fear and pity. Their eyes would quickly move from her to something else—anything else—seemingly afraid that if they rested too long upon her, they too would be struck with whatever afflicted her. She had been told not to speak to them.

They would never stop. Instead, their steps would quicken as they passed.

One day someone did stop. Elizabeth stared deeply into her sad eyes, begging for an answer. It took Elizabeth a moment to recognize her.

Rita. After all this time, Rita.

"Where have you been?" she asked. "Why did you leave me? How can I get out of this place? How did I get *into* this place? What am I doing here?" Rita just stared and said nothing. "Where have you been?" she repeated, her voice getting a bit louder and more insistent. Rita continued staring. Elizabeth began to feel a panic rise in her chest. "Why did you leave me?" she yelled, repeatedly.

Rita simply said, "I must go now." She turned and began her own walk around the circle and then she was gone.

Elizabeth had no one.

1952

When she first woke up, Elizabeth had no idea that *this* was the day. When they first entered at the end of the hallway, Elizabeth did not realize that the nurses and doctors were coming for *her*.

But they were.

For the most part, the nurses and orderlies were kind to her. She had worked in the sewing room, mindlessly filling each day with stitch after stitch, but she grew tired of creating clothes for those who were not her own. But who exactly were *hers*? And whoever they were, why had they left her in this strange place? Over and over she asked herself the same things: *To whom do I belong? Why am I here?* She found peace only when she would exhaust herself and fall to sleep, dreaming no dreams, and waking to the same endless cycle.

She told no one of her thoughts and pulled more and more into herself, seeking to find within herself what remained a mystery in the world at large. She spoke to no one, and other than the nurses, no one spoke to her.

And then, it came to her. Unbidden. A glimpse. A mere shadow of her life before. She saw a life in another place and another time, a life in the country, in a land rich with olive trees. She saw a sun that somehow seemed to be a different sun than the one in this cold place. Even the colors were different. Where once she was surrounded by warm pastel greens and tans and yellows, she was now surrounded by a cold grayness.

And another memory came to her in a flash, so dramatic it felt as if she had been shot.

Joseph! Vincent! Where were they?

That's when the torture began. She would wake up in cold dread, worried to death about Joseph and Vincent. She would look all over the ward for them. *Surely, they must be somewhere; they can't have just vanished.* She thought she would see Rita just turning a corner and hurry to catch up, eager to ask her about them. But once she had caught up, Rita had vanished. Then she understood that if she was to leave, she would have to find her own way out.

"What am I doing here? Where are they? Why have you taken them?" Most nights, the nurses would be able to comfort her, to reassure her, to get her back to sleep.

But last night was different. *Someone* had been after her. *Who* exactly had been after her? Which of the nefarious Mancinis was it? Was it Frank? Or Paolo? She sensed she was unravelling, unable to distinguish between Rita's story and her own. She thrashed about endlessly until exhaustion finally settled in. They came to her the next morning, and she knew it was her turn to go to the room where she had seen so many others go.

"We need to try something different," said the nurse. Elizabeth trusted this nurse, who was always so kind to her. At least she assumed she was a nurse—but she was not sure. Perhaps it was Rita, finally returning to find her and take her away. "We need to make the demons leave."

"But what about my sons?" Elizabeth cried.

"They will be fine," she said. "We are watching them while you get better. Just come with us."

And so she went with them. As they attached the electrodes, she began to panic, but the nurses held her down. The doctor reached over to set the dials on the front of the machine and nodded. And then there was a sudden and sharp pain. Again. Again. And again. Until there was nothing.

When she awoke, she had no idea what had happened to her. For that matter, she had no idea who she was or where she was.

The void surrounded her once again.

And the cycle would repeat.

1952

Joe sat gazing out on all the rich greenness of Yankee Stadium, pondering how lucky he was to be at the World Series.

He had always been a big baseball fan but had never quite been able to justify the cost of a World Series game. But now through the connection to the radio station at which both he and Sally worked, he had a ticket. He thumbed through the program, looking at the player's pictures and reading their biographies.

Sadly, DiMaggio wasn't in centerfield anymore. It had all came to such a bitter end during the postseason the previous year. And now Mantle, the heir apparent, was in centerfield. Joe tried to get excited about him, but he still wished that DiMaggio was out there.

Looking through the program he pondered all the alcohol and beer ads. He didn't begrudge others who liked to drink, but far too often he had seen where it could lead. When he was in the Navy, he was the one who always helped drunk sailors avoid the MPs and get them to bed. So many years had passed, but he still thought about those nights when his father would rant on and on and on, uncertain about where he might strike next and what he might do. The unpredictability is what scared him so much. And then he thought about his mother drifting off into the haze.

Joe thought about Vinnie and was glad that he was safe. He was married with a good career. He was back in New York after being on the West Coast. That was a comfort to Joe. And now he had Sally, whom he planned to marry, if she would have him, and finally have a chance to start their own family.

He wasn't sure how much to tell her about his past. He went back and forth, trying to decide what to tell her, what secrets to let out of his locked box. She was so eager for a family, as was he. But what would she think if she knew the truth about his parents?

Joe had taken Sally to meet Aunt Jennie, and they had seemed to get along well. But there were minefields there as well, not necessarily with Aunt Jennie but with the rest of the family. They all knew *exactly* what had happened to Joe's parents, but nobody was willing to talk about it. He and Vinnie were a constant reminder to all the family of the shame of everything that had happened, but no one would ever say so.

As Joe sat in the beautiful stadium, watching his beloved Yankees, he decided. Whatever few ties were left, he was going to cut them. He was not going to look back. He was going to make a fresh start with Sally. He would tuck all those memories away in the box he had been given so long ago and focus on what would come next—if Sally would have him.

FOURTEEN

There is *context* to my grandparents' story—and the secrecy around it—that is likely to feel alien to contemporary audiences, who love to talk endlessly about all sorts of afflictions, no matter how minor.

Consider, for example, the following quotes, and guess the source of each.

> (1) Gigantic sums are now required to maintain prisons and insane asylums and protect the public against gangsters and lunatics. Why do we preserve these useless and harmful beings? The abnormal prevent the development of the normal. This fact must be squarely faced. Why should society not dispose of the criminals and insane in a more economical manner?
>
> (2) [The insane] are specimens of humanity who really ought to be exterminated ... [America] must stop trying to cure malignant biological growths with patent sociological nostrums. The emergency demands a surgical operation.

(3) Apply a stern and rigid policy of sterilization and segregation to that grade of population whose progeny is tainted, or whose inheritance is such that objectionable traits may be transmitted to offspring.

Modern minds would likely attribute these kinds of sentiments to Hitler or Goebbels or Himmler. In fact, they are attributable to three Americans:

(1) Alexis Carrel, a Nobel Prize-winning physician at Rockefeller Institute for Medical Research in New York City, 1935
(2) Earnest Hooton, Harvard University, American physical anthropologist, *Apes, Men and Morons*, 1937
(3) Margaret Sanger, founder of Planned Parenthood, 1932

This kind of thinking—which ultimately reached its horrible conclusion in the Nazi death camps—didn't begin in Germany. It began in the United Kingdom and the United States with the eugenics movement. Eugenics is the idea that inferior groups of people (such as deformed, mentally disabled, and certain races) should be culled from the human population. The term is attributed to nineteenth-century British anthropologist Francis Galton, although the concept goes back millennia.

Robert Whitaker notes in *Mad in America* that the eugenics movement spread quickly in the United States:

The American Eugenics Society (AES) was incorporated in 1926. John D. Rockefeller Jr. contributed $10,000 to help launch it. George Eastman, of Eastman Kodak fame, gave $20,000. Yale professor Irving Fisher, the best-known economist of his time, served as the first president. In a short period, it grew into a truly national organization, with chapters in twenty-eight states…

From the beginning, American eugenicists had a clear-cut agenda for preventing the mentally ill from having children. States would need to make it illegal for the insane to marry, segregate them into asylums, and release them only after they had been sterilized. Only then would they cease to be a threat to the country's genetic makeup.

All these forces combined to reverse the tide of moral care for the mentally ill initiated by the Quakers and codified by Thomas Story Kirkbride in the nineteenth century, the tide of care that had created institutions like Buffalo and Rockland.

By the 1920s and 1930s, Americans were *done* with the idea of moral care. They were *done* with the notion of individually caring for the mentally ill and helping them move back into the mainstream. By the 1920s and 1930s, Americans were intent on removing "malignant poisonous growths" (Earnest Hooten) from their midst and were focused on simply warehousing the mentally ill—preferably somewhere out of sight.

My grandparents were confronted by a society not only fearful of their Italian "otherness" and the diluting of the purity of the American-Northern European "race," but also one intent on removing the "mentality unfit" from the mainstream of society. The mindset of the times made it very difficult for my grandparents. Their ethnicity disrupted the purity objectives of the eugenics crowd—a crowd that was far more mainstream than we would care to admit. Add poverty to the mix, and you have a trifecta of awful possibilities.

The result was life sentences in underfunded and understaffed and overcrowded facilities for many who did not fit the proper mold of "normalness." With this in mind, my family's shame—and all the secrets that surrounded that shame—are a bit easier to understand.

Whatever the explanation, Frank and Elizabeth sank into the quicksand and disappeared.

A key question remains—what eventually happened to Frank and Elizabeth? How long did they live after being committed and when did they die?

My efforts to acquire a death certificate were stymied for quite some time by the fact that I did not have a place of death or even an approximate date of death, and New York State refused to release any of my grandparents' health records.

That was until my genealogical savant brother Joe sends me this Facebook message: "Here's something that turned up on Ancestry that blew my mind. It's from a Social Security applications and claims file on Ancestry.com. Get ready." I held my breath for whatever was coming next. "I think I found Frank's record in that file and if I'm right, he lived until 1990 and died somewhere in NYC."

The birthdate for my grandfather isn't exactly right, but a lot of the other information matched.

Joe and I are in shock. We can't believe this date of death—it just seems too extraordinary to be true. Going from thinking that both my grandparents died in a fire in the 1930s to my grandfather Frank possibly being alive through 1990—*without any of us knowing anything*—seems impossible. This certainly couldn't be correct.

Armed with the proposed 1990 death date for Frank, I order a copy of the actual death certificate, and my brother uncovers another medical record from Rockland. The admission date to Rockland matches the previous records we had uncovered: 17 August 1932.

The 13 July 1990, *discharge* date (he was discharged to the American Nursing Home on Avenue B in New York) means Frank spent almost *fifty-seven years* at the Rockland Asylum. The discharge notes are perhaps one of the saddest postscripts to a life that I've ever heard.

> This is a 91-year-old ambulatory male admitted to Rockland Psychiatric Center at the age of 35 years with a diagnosis of schizophrenia, paranoid type. At that time, he was hallucinating and delusional with impaired insight and judgement. Over the years he was tried on various neuroleptics, but there was no steady improvement ... Patient is kept in a geri-chair most of the time because if left ambulatory he rubs his face with dirty linen and drinks water from the toilet bowl. He is mute and cannot make his needs known. He is very thin (104 pounds) and is

not in touch with reality. Remote and recent memory cannot be tested. Insight and judgment are nil, and he appears completely disoriented.

When Frank's death certificate arrives, it confirms he died in 1990—on July 16, to be specific.

Frank was buried in Calvary Cemetery in Queens. Calvary is noteworthy because it has the largest number of interments—3 million—of any cemetery in the country. Every time we went past a crowded cemetery when I was growing up, my father used to say, "People are just dying to get in there."

Calvary seems oddly familiar to me and then I remember having seen it on an Ancestry.com record. Michael (Frank's brother) and the beloved Aunt Jennie *are also buried there.*

Is this a long-lost family connection for Frank? Maybe Frank wasn't as alone and abandoned as I had thought. When I call the cemetery, however, they tell me the two plots were completely unrelated. They say that Frank was buried in a "free" section of the cemetery, essentially the Potter's Field portion of Calvary. He is in Section 1-W, Avenue M, Plot 28, Grave 11. In an unmarked grave.

As I make plans to go find this place, I recall that I was born in Queens, where we originally lived before relocating to New Jersey. When I ask my mom where exactly we lived after I was born, she tells me it was a railway flat, an apartment consisting of a series of rooms connected to each other in a line, like a railway car. After a bit of prodding, she remembers that the apartment was just off Queens Boulevard, along the subway line, and that the cross street was likely 48th or 49th.

My grandfather Francesco Mancini came to the United States from Italy in 1921. He never returned. Almost exactly a century later *to the day,* I am standing at his grave. Truth be told, I am only *approximately* at his grave given that unmarked graves are, well, unmarked. I type Queens Boulevard and 48th Street into my Google Maps. It turns out I am standing less than a mile from my parents' first apartment, the first place where I lived.

What a long, strange family trip it has been.

But what about Elizabeth?

The same Social Security record as the one we discover for Frank also has a possible date of death for Elizabeth, which we use to request a death certificate from New York State.

After about a month, we get her death certificate from New York State. She died on 16 February 2002. *She was over one hundred years old.*

Somehow, she wound up back near where she started—New York City—but we have no real idea how she got there, and New York State refuses to release any records.

On the positive side, I seem to have hit the jackpot for longevity genes. But that's easily outweighed by the over 121 collective years of insanity and incarceration.

Elizabeth's death certificate says she is buried in Colonial Memorial Park, outside *Trenton*. The website notes that "Colonial Memorial Park is a beautiful historic cemetery located in Hamilton Township serving all of Mercer County." Their mission statement is an ambitious one: "Caring for Families ... Eternally."

Armed with this information, I call Colonial Memorial Park to see if there is any information on where in the cemetery Elizabeth is buried and more importantly, who had made the arrangements. I think maybe there might be some family connection of which none of us are aware. Sadly, it turns out that Elizabeth's arrangements were also made by the court. According to the person at the cemetery, this was a normal procedure for indigent people with no obvious relatives.

Elizabeth's final destination was Hamilton, New Jersey, a little more than one hundred years after her birth in Itri, Italy. Quite a journey. She never made it back home to Italy. She never saw her children grow up. I am unsure why a court in Queens would send someone to a cemetery outside of Trenton, but there are obviously no Interstate Commerce Commission restrictions on shipping dead people across state lines.

On a cold and rainy day in May, my wife and I head to Colonial Memorial Park on our way home from a trip to visit our daughter in New York City. After exiting I-295, we head south on State Route 206. SR-106 seems oddly familiar—although I had never been to that cemetery—and then I realize why. About sixteen miles north, SR-206 connects to Nassau Street in Princeton. During my two years at Princeton, Elizabeth was still alive somewhere. Neither of us had any idea that her final unmarked resting place would be just a few miles down the road.

As we approach the cemetery, we drive past a collection of fast-food hamburger joints, a Walgreens, and Anthony's Pizza Palace. Perhaps my Italian immigrant grandmother would take some solace that her final resting place is just a stone's throw from the Pizza Palace, rated 4.5 out of 5 by Google. "Murals line the walls of this casual, long-running pizza parlor serving Italian comfort foods" a review stated. My GPS chirps to announce that a Dunkin Donuts was ahead on the right and that the cemetery would be next.

The cemetery has been in business for more than a century and frankly is a little worn around the edges. Not that my grandmother likely cares.

The grounds are centered around a huge oval drive. Most of the graves have upright markers and some have markers flush to the ground. We drive through a pretty canopy of trees on both sides of a road bisecting the oval and parked near a tall obelisk resembling a lighthouse. Following the directions given me via email from the Colonial staff, I walk through the drizzle and find Elizabeth's grave.

The graves in that part of the cemetery are unmarked, but that day my grandmother's is marked with a little blue marker, courtesy of the cemetery staff. Her nearest neighbor with an actual gravestone is about one hundred feet away, Leon McClendon, a.k.a. "Booda," born on 16 May 1987. The inscription notes that he was a loving son, brother, and father. He passed from this earthly vale on 25 July 2015. He was twenty-eight years old. There are some pretty purple flowers in front of his tombstone, the only tombstone in a vast field of unmarked graves.

While I would like to feel great sadness at Elizabeth's pathetic and anonymous blue stake, I suppose Booda's stone reminds me that there is always more than enough sadness to go around in this world.

And no one has a monopoly on sadness.

FIFTEEN

I have a new love for that glittering instrument, the human soul. It is a lovely and unique thing in the universe. It is always attacked and never destroyed—because "Thou mayest." (John Steinbeck, East of Eden)

I don't pretend to understand the pain that goes along with a violent childhood home and the loss of not one but *both* parents—and a loss that does not have the finality of death but occurs somewhere in the no-man's land of a pair of lifetime sentences to a pair of insane asylums.

I realize that on one level my quest has been about trying to find my grandparents. The tragedy of simply drifting unknown and unloved into the backwaters of history is just too much for me to accept.

But really, this whole thing has also been about my search for my father, to better understand who and whose he was. My father was kind and non-judgmental and quick with a joke, even those jokes that were made at his own expenses.

So how do I reconcile this person with the one whose parents were *alive for over half a century each*, and he not only never visited them but *never even mentioned them*? How does such a thing happen? How do they just vanish?

The story of family madness—and my father's reaction to that madness—does not end there.

My father's younger brother Vincent was strikingly handsome and an artist. As a kid, I can remember family gatherings with Uncle Vinnie and his wife and kids. Many years after it occurred, I discovered that my uncle had some sort of breakdown. He tried to commit suicide. He made threats against our family. And so, he too vanished from the family history.

My last memory of my uncle is going with my father to visit him at an institution or hospital of some sort when I was ten years old. I can still remember him incessantly squeezing a rubber ball as some sort of stress reliever.

Squeeze. Release. Squeeze. Release.

Three of my father's closest family members—mother, father, and brother—all disappeared without a trace into mental health institutions . . . *for the rest of their lives.* Three lives, 162 years lived in anonymity in institutions, vanishing without a trace as though they never lived. Along with the disappearance of these three closest family members came the disappearance of this entire side of the family.

As kids we used to joke that if we ever went to a restaurant in which the meal was below par, my Irish mother would want to complain loudly. My Italian father, however, would simply say, "That's alright. We just won't come back here anymore."

My father had to endure a lot in life. First his parents were institutionalized when he was young and then thirty years later his brother careened down the same slippery slope. How do you cope with such incredible pain? The descent of my uncle into the same schizophrenia that claimed his parents and shaped his childhood must have scared him to death. I can't imagine. *And he never said anything.* At least to any of us. I wonder about the strain that maintaining this code of secrecy took on him, and whether that had something to do with his early death at sixty-two.

Dani Shapiro is a best-selling writer who started the *Dani Shapiro Family Secrets* podcast about stories from guests who discover long-hidden secrets from their families' past. In one episode a former CIA spy talks about the challenge of being undercover in Shanghai in an apartment that was under constant surveillance 24 hours per day, 7 days per week. The former agent describes the cumulative strain of maintaining her covert identity without release:

> What's it like to live your life so deep undercover, handling secrets that are so sensitive, not even the people who know you best—not your friends, not your siblings, not your parents—can know what you're up to? Ex-CIA agent Amaryllis Fox spent the better part of her 20s trying to keep WMDs out of the hands of global terror groups—until she became a mother and realized she couldn't ask her baby daughter to live inside a secret world.

In his induction papers during World War II, my father listed stamp collecting as one of his hobbies. As a kid, I remember helping him soak stamps off envelopes. I never thought about the solitary nature of this hobby and how it could provide the basis for escape. I never thought about how it likely gave him a sense of order, each stamp with a number and a picture in an album, the goals neatly laid out in a set of pictures on a page in a Scott's Album, each waiting to be covered by the corresponding stamp. Those books gave him a perfect world, everything in order.

Elania Gil, a well-known expert on childhood trauma, emailed me some insights that seem so on point for my father:

> Collecting stamps is a solitary yet connected activity. It allows the creative imagination to soar. Stamps come from different places and go to other places, they are mobile, they are valuable, they carry important information. They can also be overlooked, or their role minimized by others. Imagine the act of selecting them out for attention, carefully and gently caring for them, keeping them intact, placing them in order, giving them their value and their place in life. I can imagine this could have been a huge metaphor for your father, far beyond what the naked eye could see. The organization, the order, the chronicling in time and space, was relevant to him. But the other part was the intentionality to value something that has a huge value and purpose (nothing can move without its presence), but then is often overlooked, disregarded, and finally, discarded by many. I get chills thinking about how important and relevant this activity might have been to a man who had felt the absence of value, because his parents were not capable of providing that (email from Ms. Gil).

IMMIGRANT SECRETS

There are two episodes in Malcolm Gladwell's *Revisionist History* podcast that particularly strike home when I think about my father's story. "Carlos Doesn't Remember" is about the incredible waste of human potential among talented kids with "challenging" backgrounds. Carlos was an exceptionally talented kid from the projects who faced all sorts of obstacles to fulfilling his potential. Kids like that—poor kids, often from immigrant backgrounds—do not get the second chances that kids from privilege do.

How do these kids survive? Gladwell notes:

> Even as an 8-year-old, this kid was smart enough to know that ... his job was to put all the bad stuff aside, to put it in a box. That's what these kids are like, the ones who make it out. They learn from a very early age where the exits are and they don't let anything get in their way (Malcolm Gladwell, "Carlos Doesn't Remember," Revisionist History podcast, season 1, episode 4, 2016)

I think more than anything, *that* is the best explanation for how my father survived.

The second Gladwell episode that comes to mind is the "Basement Tapes," recorded in 2017 and which deals with people discovering unexpected information about a loved one after their death. It was especially poignant given that Gladwell's own father had just passed away.

How do you deal with the discovery of information that is inconsistent with the experience that you have always known? How do you talk about it? Is it better to just shut up? These are questions I have also pondered on this family quest. Gladwell notes:

I took my father's presence for granted for as long as he was alive and when he died, the first shocking realization was that I had to find a way to keep him alive in my heart, to honor his memory. How do we do that? Not by honoring our parents' beliefs, we are different people than they are, born in different eras, shaped by different forces. What we are obliged to honor in our parents is their principles, the rules by which they lived their lives. (Malcolm Gladwell, "Basement Tapes," Revisionist History podcast, season 2, episode 10, 2017)

My father gave us the gift of stability that he never had. We grew up in the New Jersey suburbs and had the kind of second chances resulting from privilege that kids like Carlos don't get. I don't think we ever appreciated what a gift that was until my brother and I started probing around our family history.

My sister June believes, "It must have been something he compartmentalized and put deeply away. Maybe he knew initially what happened but then didn't pursue it." Joe adds, "From age five to seven, Dad's father was going down the path of mental illness. His father was crazy, crazy and abusive. Back then people didn't talk about any of this and actively worked to keep things like this hidden."

My brother and I debated whether to raise all this secret history with our mom and ultimately decide that telling the story is a way to keep my father's story alive. We wonder about what to ask our mom about all of this, and what she knew. June says that in graduate school she needed to develop a family history as part of her child psychology degree:

I had a chart with all these empty spaces. So, I called Mom and asked her about Dad's family. It seemed to be a distressing thing for her, so I kind of abandoned it. My first instinct was that she was protecting information. But at some point, I concluded that it was just an embarrassing thing for her to admit that she was married to this person for so many years and never knew any of this.

My sister Jeanne thinks that my mom probably knew things but has forgotten them or is simply too embarrassed to admit that she didn't know. "You know how Mom just loves to *know* stuff. She always likes to think that she has the inside information. I think it's embarrassing to her to think that she was married to somebody for over thirty years and never thought to ask him about any of this." My brother Jeff says, "I was in my mid-twenties and Dad had passed away by the time I found out he *even had a brother* ... I think most people have doors inside of them that are just not to be opened."

After Harry Potter prevails in the Chamber of Secrets, Harry Potter spoke to Dumbledore in his office. Harry worries aloud about the similarities he notices between himself and Tom Riddle, and Dumbledore responds, "It is our *choices* that show what we truly are, far more than our abilities."[5] Choices. I think it ultimately all comes down to choices.

In *East of Eden*, John Steinbeck talks about the choice we all get between good and evil. He uses the Cain and Abel story as the central metaphor for the book. About half-way through

---

5 J.K. Rowling, *Harry Potter and the Chamber of Secrets,* London: Pottermore Publishing, 1998)

the book, there is a key conversation between Samuel Trask and the "pidgin English speaking but secretly wiser than everyone else" servant Lee. It provides the very core of the book.[6]

It turns out that Lee and a group of Chinese elders became so preoccupied with the story of Cain and Abel that they decide to learn Hebrew to better understand the core message of the text. And according to Steinbeck, when God confronts Cain with the death of his brother Abel, everything comes down to a single word, *timshel*.

> Don't you see?" he [Lee] cried. "The American Standard translation orders men to triumph over sin, and you can call sin ignorance. The King James translation makes a promise in "Thou shalt," meaning that men will surely triumph over sin.
>
> But the Hebrew word, the word *timshel* — "Thou mayest"—that gives a choice. It might be the most important word in the world. That says the way is open. That throws it right back on a man. For if "Thou mayest," it is also true that "Thou mayest not." Don't you see?...
>
> Now, there are many millions in their sects and churches who feel the order, "Do thou," and throw their weight into obedience. And there are millions more who feel predestination in "Thou shalt." Nothing they may do can interfere with what will be.

---

6   John Steinbeck, *East of Eden*. New York: Penguin Books, 2017.

But "Thou mayest"! Why, that makes a man great, that gives him stature with the gods... He can choose his course and fight it through and win.

Ever since I first read that book—and I have re-read it many times since—that passage has gone to my core, and I never knew why. I never realized it was the story of my father's life.

Thou *shall*, and you have no free will, because your actions are commanded.

Thou *will*, and you also have no free will. All the choices are already made for you; everything is predetermined.

But thou *mayest*. That's the gray area in which we all ultimately live. That's the place where courage and fear and uncertainty lie. And I suppose that's what being human is ultimately all about.

I am not saying that my father and his brother were Cain and Abel. But the central point of the story—that we each make a choice about our redemption, that it's a *choice*, not a command or an inevitability—is, I think, central to my father's story.

My father survived the tragedy of his childhood the only way he knew—by roping off his pain in a tight box and by resolving to never go back there again. And when his brother descended into the same place as his parents, my father reached back into the only experience he had, and seeing the wife and six kids he needed to protect, decided again that he would not go back there. It's not the choice everyone would make, and it's probably not completely understandable in our current world in which so very few things are held secret. But it was a choice. *Thou mayest.*

My father was the child of poor immigrants who spoke little English. He grew up with an often-violent father. His parents struggled to maintain their sanity in the middle of the Great Depression. When they failed, with nowhere else to turn, his mother committed his father to an asylum. And then six years later, she followed him. Never to be heard from again. And to add insult to injury, his own brother followed the same tragic path.

Dr. Eliana Gil e-mailed me something that means the world to me. I suppose in many ways it captures the weird, unassuming, and quiet heroism that must have been at the center of my father's life. By trying to understand this, maybe I can free my father and free my grandparents from the prison of their insanity:

> Working with parents who have had traumatic pasts, I can also tell you that the determining factor in many cases, is the CONSCIOUS CHOICE to change something for self and others, and not repeat past traumas. Most people can't do this, instead, they repeat their histories and bring their past traumas into their current lives. They relive the traumas, and they are driven by unconscious behavioral re-enactments. *There is great strength in choosing to do something different.*

Not every *timshel* choice is perfect. Not every *timshel* choice is the one that I might make. But as Atticus said, "You never really understand a person until you consider things from his point of view… until you climb in his skin and walk around in it."[7]

Timshel.

---

7 Harper Lee, To Kill a Mockingbird. 40th Anniversary ed., New York: HarperCollins Publishers, 1999

SIXTEEN

*"In which direction does the light reside?
And where is the place of darkness?" (Job 38:19)*

JOSEPH JOHN MANCINI (1925-1987)

*Ninna nanna, ninna oh
Questo bimbo a chi lo do?*
Lullaby, lullaby, lullaby, oh
Who will I give this baby to?

Joseph gazed at the tiny points of light, lights that offered promise . . . and peace. Lights that offered home.

As he drifted toward the lights, he seemed to be going inconceivably fast and at the same time agonizingly slow. He had always known of these lights, but they were always beyond his grasp deep within himself.

All that was changing now.

He prayed that he would know, and that he would be known.

Waves of consciousness engulfed Joseph. He was at once both part of the wave and yet distinct from it. He waited for the wave to crest. As the wave crashed against the shore, He saw it all. His whole life, each moment captured. All the confusion and blank spaces vanished. He no longer saw through a glass dimly.

And he was aware of other waves, waves that had preceded his. Michael. Jennie. Michele. Teresa. Domenico. Maria. Adrianna.

There were others still behind him, yet to come. Vincent. Francesco. Elisabetta. And a host of other waves, indistinct in the distance, each separate but part of the same ocean.

Ninna oh ninna oh
A nessuno lo daro.
Lullaby, lullaby, lullaby, oh
To no one I'll give you, my treasure.

He was surrounded by the lights. He was known.

EPILOGUE

Roughly speaking, for everything that could be considered a historical fact in this book, I made something up — and I'd like to think that a lot of the time readers won't be able to tell the difference.

(Kate Atkinson, Transcription)

In 1932, on the heels of a five day stay at Bellevue Hospital that was triggered by multiple incidents of abusive behavior, my grandfather Francesco was certified "indigent" and "insane." He then spent the rest of his life (until 1990) at the Rockland Asylum. My grandmother Elisabetta survived another six years on the "outside," ultimately succumbing to the pressures of life as a single parent immigrant in the Great Depression and earning her own commitment prize in 1938, after a mere six days at Bellevue. She, too, spent the rest of her life institutionalized.

New York State refuses all these years later to release any of their medical records due to "privacy" concerns. With no one to ask – my father died in 1987 – we're left wondering what exactly happened between 1938 and their deaths in 1990 and

2002. Over 121 years of my grandparents' lives were spent institutionalized and forgotten. That's more than 44,000 days. I suppose in some way, this book—in addition to being about the search for my father and his parents—is also a plea that New York State and all the other states with similar outdated records policies make their records public and allow the many families like ours some peace. It's time.

I originally set out to find out as much as I could about this strange pair of immigrants. I did not want them to be lost forever. Hitting a dead end and not knowing more about their lives after they were institutionalized leaves a void. It feels akin to losing a loved one. It leaves a gap in our origins story. Their lives were tragic enough. But for their lives to be unchronicled or even acknowledged made the tragedy infinitely worse. I wanted to breathe a bit of life into them so that they would not continue to be lost, but at least partially found.

St. Rita of Cascia is real—well, among Catholics at least—as is her marriage to a nefarious Mancini and also Rita's sacrifice to save her two sons. But as similar as their lives might have been, I don't know whether there was any connection between Rita and Elisabetta other than to help me tell the story of my grandmother's descent.

The Archie Leach part of the conversation between Elisabetta and Archie was drawn directly from _Archie Leach_ by Cary Grant. And yes, he was on the ship with my grandmother, but I have no idea if they ever met.

I don't know whether Elisabetta ever had electroshock treatment, although as I note in the text, it was a common treatment for those diagnosed with dementia praecox.

Everything else in this book is true—or could be—and mostly factual.

I think we sometimes arrogantly forget that even tragic lives leave a footprint, a legacy. It is tempting to dismiss the lives of Francesco and Elisabetta and people like them as meaningless. They were immigrants who wound up institutionalized for most of their lives, contributing little to society. There are many cold people in our current world who look at the stream of immigrants at our border or those desperate to escape from Kabul or The Ukraine and think these poor souls have little to contribute.

However, there is a longer arc to every story, one that is equally important. The legacy of Francesco and Elisabetta—tragic though their lives were—is one that would have amazed them.

2 sons.
Joseph
Vincent

9 grandchildren.
John
June
Joseph
Jennifer
Jeffrey
Jeanne
Vincent
Victor
Carla

21 great grandchildren.
    Joseph
    William
    Erin
    Christopher
    Daniel
    Kathryn
    Kelly
    Katelyn
    Chrissy
    Jimmy
    Leann
    Emily
    Douglas
    Rebecca
    Brian
    Ben
    Michael
    Melissa
    Cameron
    Andrea
    Christian

16 great great grandchildren.
    Claire
    Grace
    Emma
    Nora

Jack
Lucy
Alex
Declan
Carson
Harper
Palmer
Devon
Ella
Audry
Liam
Arlo

And counting.

SOURCES AND ACKNOWLEDGEMENTS

A sampling of some of my original source documents can be found at http://www.searchformygrandparents.com.

Many thanks to my brother Joseph for his equal zeal for this weird genealogical project. Some of the story has been condensed into an "I" to make the story-telling easier, when it might have been more accurate to say "Joseph" or "we."

I know there is a big debate in the genealogy community about what should be freely available and what is only available behind the Ancestry.com paywall. I do know that many of the documents and connections central to our story could only have been found through Ancestry. I am still hoping that Ancestry DNA will uncover some cousins in Itri or the US who miraculously have some childhood pictures maybe lost in a trunk for over a century waiting for someone who cares.

I am also grateful for the contributions to our collective family history provided by Donna DeFabritus Binzer, whom I have never met and never even knew existed but is *family* and shares my obsession with documenting our origins. If I am doing the math properly, she is my second cousin. Her grandfather was Dominick, Elizabeth's brother. Donna connected my mother, brother, and me with her Aunt Frances Sinapi—Dominick's daughter—whom we also never knew existed but was my father's first cousin and knew him. My dad and his brother lived with them for a time before he went into the Navy.

We had a memorable lunch on Staten Island with Frances. At the time, Frances was a spunky ninety-five-plus-year-old, living by herself on Staten Island. We didn't discuss a lot of the family history because we didn't know a lot of it at the time. But the lunch was a hoot, and it was amazing to connect with an actual relative on the Italian side. She shared with us a picture from her brother's wedding in 1951 that included my Uncle Vinnie (6th from the right), and a tall fellow named Alex Kotwas, peeking Kilroy-esque over the rest of the celebrants.

Alex was a lifelong friend of my father's. He was at my parents' wedding. A few years after my father died and after Alex's wife died, my mother and Alex got together and eventually married. But *that's* a story for another day. I so wish I had asked him what he knew about my father's story when he was still around.

For those just starting out on your ancestry journey, make sure to check out genealogy groups on Facebook. A huge thank you to the folks in the Italian genealogy groups on Facebook who helped me with finding my grandfather's World War I military records and translating various Italian records. I vow to learn Italian someday as penance.

So many of the asylums that were set up with such good "Kirkbride" intentions toward the end of the 19th century wound up overwhelmed and overcrowded by rising numbers and shrinking public funds. It is inspiring to read about these early pioneers in the treatment of mental illness, and yet it's a shame how far we have fallen from their vision.

It is easy to feel outrage at the institutionalizing of those who found themselves on the fringes of society and/or sanity. So much of the history of these institutions has remained intentionally hidden, the subject only of horror film movie plots. The Buffalo State Asylum and Hospital Facebook page is a striking exception, and the insights on that page often serve as a reminder to examine our own behavior with regards to mental illness. Far too often, we just turn people who need help onto the streets or drug them. How does this standard of care compare to that of the Kirkbride pioneers?

For Annie—last name unknown—at the Immaculate Conception Church in lower Manhattan (which absorbed the Mary Help of Christians Church after it was torn down) who found the marriage record for my grandparents that finally revealed their *actual birth dates*... and two sets of great grandparents. I owe you. The power of records is amazing.

Steve Luxenberg (author of *Annie's Ghosts*) put me onto an invaluable idea—searching for commitment records as an end-run around health record restrictions. And thanks to Libby Copeland (author of *The Lost Family*) for turning me on to the records potential of the New York Society for the Prevention of Cruelty to Children (NYSPCC).

Which brings me to the NYSPCC's Chelsea Frank. I am so grateful to her for uncovering the records that FINALLY told the story of how my grandmother wound up committed. You were like the cavalry riding in at the last minute when I had given up hope of ever finding out what happened.

I am still amazed that Jamie Ford (author of the fabulous book *Hotel on the Corner of Bitter and Sweet*) responded to my Facebook message early one Sunday morning *within an hour*, offering encouragement and directing me to *Characters & Viewpoint* by Orson Scott Card. I so wish I could write like Jamie.

When I was running out of steam during COVID, I came across Dani Shapiro's *Inheritance* (thank you, MG for the referral) and her podcast *Family Secrets*, and so appreciate the inspiration. I even got to be one of those mystery recorded voices for audience submitted stories that she runs between seasons of her podcast.

Dr. Eliana Gil is one of the foremost authorities in the world on child trauma; many people know that. But I can also say that she is one of the *nicest* people as well. Out of the blue, I contacted her to ask her whether my thoughts about how my dad dealt with trauma were on target or not. She contacted me *less than ninety minutes* after I emailed her, providing incredible insights and encouragement. I still find that hard to believe; I need to do *much* better when people contact me looking for help on document management and records management issues.

Projects like this swirl around in your head for a long time. When you finally get down to putting words to paper—or I guess more accurately, electrons to screen—you agitate a long time about even telling anyone what you are up to for fear of looking foolish. Once this project got into book form, thank you for the gentle editing and prodding of Geoffrey Stone, and the cover and interior artistry of Danna Mathias.

I am so grateful to my wife, Mary Glenn, who has been supportive of this weird enterprise every step of the way. It was *her* extended family that first got me interested in family history, because there wasn't much *history* on my side, not to mention very much in the way of *family*. There are a host of interesting family stories on her side that need attention.

Thanks to my parents and my sibs—June, Joseph, Jennifer, Jeff, and Jeanne—for being the family growing up that my father never had. Yes, we are weird. Very weird. But we know it and we laugh a lot, even if we repeat the same jokes over and over and over. I owe bonus sib points to my partner in genealogy crime brother Joe and my sister June for looking at some early drafts.

And thank you to my niece Leann Carroll (she immediately "got" the point of the book *exactly*), and friends Linda Johnson Wood (the first brave reader other than Mary Glenn!), family history savants Kristin Brown and Mary Sue Magee Hunt, Joe Ryan (*pages* of notes and the advice to open up a bit more, never an easy thing for me), Dan Antion, Judi Elmore, Jim Williams (he is responsible for the title and will be in charge of casting for the movie), Craig Shogren, Sean McGauley, and

Larry Wischerth. They all took seriously my desire to write all of this down, read drafts of this book, and were willing to spend time telling me what they thought.

Dibs on Tom Hanks playing me and Meryl Streep playing MG in the movie.

Timshel.

SELECTED BIBLIOGRAPHY

Buffalo State Hospital, *Annual Report*, 1944.

Card, Orson Scott. *Characters & Viewpoint*. Writer's Digest Books, 2010.

Carr, Nick. "Scouting An Abandoned Mental Asylum: A Visit to the Rockland Psychiatric Center, Parts 1 and 2." *Scouting NY*, 9 Jan. 2014, www.scoutingny.com/scouting-an-abandoned-mental-asylum-a-visit-to-the-rockland-psychiatric-center-part-1/.

Chirnside, Mark. *RMS Olympic: Titanic's Sister*. The History Press, 2015.

Conte, Bernadette. *Eviva Maria Madonna Della Civita: the Eternal Bond of the Itrani Immigrants of Cranston, Rhode Island with Their Homeland of Itri, Italy, and Their Unwavering Faith to the Madonna*. Xlibris Corp, 2014.

Copeland, Libby. *Lost Family: How DNA Testing Is Upending Who We Are*. Harry N. Abrams, 2021.

Dorney, John. *Peace after the Final Battle: The Story of the Irish Revolution, 1912-1924*. New Island, 2020.

Evans, Rachel Held. *Inspired: Slaying Giants, Walking on Water, and Loving the Bible Again*. Thomas Nelson Publishers, 2018.

Farley, Doug. *Buffalo State Hospital: a History of the Institution in Light and Shadow*. Museum of DisABILITY History, 2015.

Ford, Jamie. *Hotel on the Corner of Bitter and Sweet*. Ballantine Books, 2019.

Gil, Eliana. *Outgrowing the Pain: A Book for and about Adults Abused as Children*. Dell Publishers, 1988.

Gladwell, Malcolm. "Basement Tapes" and "Carlos Doesn't Remember," *Revisionist History*, www.pushkin.fm/show/revisionist-history/.

Grant, Cary. "Cary Grant Autobiography - The Ultimate Cary Grant Pages," *Archie Leach by Cary Grant*. www.carygrant.net/autobiography/autobiography1.html.

H. E. Harris and Company. *Ivory Stamp Club with Captain Tim Healy*. 1934.

IMDb.com "Seventh Heaven." IMDb, 25 Mar. 1937, www.imdb.com/title/tt0029539/.

IMDb.com "The Snake Pit." IMDb, 1948, https://www.imdb.com/title/tt0040806/.

Luxenberg, Steve. *Annie's Ghosts: a Journey into a Family Secret*. Hachette Books, 2014.

Miller, Stuart, and Angela Voulangas. *A Tenement Story: The History of 97 Orchard Street and the Lower East Side Tenement Museum*. Lower East Side Tenement Museum, 2008.

New York State Education Department. *Preliminary Guide to Mental Health Documentary Sources in New York State*. 2000.

Penney, Darby, and Peter Stastny. *The Lives They Left behind: Suitcases from a State Hospital Attic*. Bellevue Literary Press, 2010.

Rutherford, Adam. *A Brief History of Everyone Who Ever Lived: the Stories in Our Genes*. Weidenfeld & Nicolson, 2017.

Shapiro, Dani. *Inheritance: A Memoir of Genealogy, Paternity, and Love.* Anchor Books, 2020.

Steinbeck, John. *East of Eden.* Penguin Books, 2017.

Whitaker, Robert. *Mad in America: Bad Science, Bad Medicine, and the Enduring Mistreatment of the Mentally Ill.* Basic Books, 2019.

Ziegelman, Jane. *97 Orchard: an Edible History of Five Immigrant Families in One New York Tenement.* JHSFC, 2012.

Printed in Great Britain
by Amazon